TANGERINE

NAMITA
DEVIDAYAL

TANGERINE

How to Read the Upanishads Without Giving Up Coffee

WESTLAND
NON·FICTION

WESTLAND
NON·FICTION

Published by Westland Non-Fiction, an imprint of Westland Books, a division of Nasadiya Technologies Private Limited, in 2025

No. 269/2B, First Floor, 'Irai Arul', Vimalraj Street, Nethaji Nagar, Alapakkam Main Road, Maduravoyal, Chennai 600095

ISBN: 9789360451325

10 9 8 7 6 5 4 3 2

Typeset by Jojy Philip

Printed at Thomson Press (India) Ltd

For those entering the forest

CONTENTS

INTRODUCTION

We live in chaotic times. Many of the certitudes we held to be sacrosanct are disintegrating. Our home, this glorious planet, is in peril and, across the world, a tsunami of hatred is drowning out reason. Has progress made us any happier? Or wiser? But that is at the macro level. In my own life, there came a point when I fell into a slump. The usual places held no palliative answers. So, I became an accidental spiritual archaeologist and, paradoxically, discovered that going inwards helped make sense of the outside.

Thanks to a friend nudging me, I turned my biases on mute, stopped hesitating, and began my journey of self-discovery through an exploration of the essence of Hindu philosophy. Hinduism may be fifty shades and more of tangerine, but I gradually started discovering that there is an underlying metaphysical idea that underscores the unity of all beings. The essence of this philosophy is that you can only change the self, and that is the real purpose of life. You don't even have to be Hindu to follow it. Also, and I hardly need to say it, there is very little connection between this philosophy and Hindutva.

In the beginning, I wondered why I continually sought something so radically different from my rational, modern, individual-focused, Western-educated belief system. But the deeper I dug, the more I realised that matter and spirit need not be in opposition. A leaf's symmetry, and indeed the whole universe, can be viewed through the scientific lens as well as with a sense of wonder that bows to the creativity of all existence. Reason and faith do not have to be positioned as binaries.

This book is about aligning with my tangerine heartbeat. It is a walk on the wild side, into an ageless anonymous wisdom that endures beyond the human. As I look back at my childhood, marriage, various adventurous excursions and connect the dots, I am understanding the map of my life. And I repeatedly return to the sweet, funny myths about Ganesha and Hanuman, and the boatman who told Prince Rama that they were both doing the same thing: helping people cross over to the other side ...

THE ROPE AND THE SNAKE

You see something in the dark. It seems to be a snake, so you jump with terror. But it's a rope.

This story has a real part and an unreal part. 'There is something'—that part is real. It is absolute and irrefutable. The 'snake' is unreal, but only relatively so, because it does bring on fear and makes you want to run.

Now, when you shine light on this object, the real part 'there is' remains unchanged, but the unreal 'snake' changes to a 'rope'. Suddenly, the perception—which was the mind's projection—changes. This is how most of us live. In a state of constant fear of what may not be real.

The snake–rope paradox is the great mystery of our lives. We cannot say it is there, nor that it is not there. On one level, it is there, because we really did jump with terror. On another, it is not there, because what made us jump was a mere rope.

What we see is, therefore, not the whole truth. The sky is not blue, and the sun does not really set in the ocean. Our thoughts and senses offer only one dimension of experiencing the world. We superimpose our ideas, often from a confused, cluttered or curdled mindspace, turning many ropes into snakes. When the light shines, we realise that there is no snake. The only absolute truth is: 'there is … there is … there is'.

The lesson: Operate in the world with the knowledge that you are the individual who may see the rope as the snake, but you also know that it is not real. That perspective, and the pause it entails, enables the 'is' to unfold in all its divine perfection.

– From the Mandukya Upanishad

ISS PAAR

CROSSING THE RIVER

The secret of water is that it is
everywhere—in the glaciers, in a pond,
in a jug of water, in a cloud
and in our bodies.
It is always present. It only changes its form.

THE TURNING POINT

So, how did I find myself on the banks of the Ganga on my birthday? And why did I come to pay heed to this unusual stream of knowledge that flowed down through the centuries like the river?

Let me rewind a little.

I was happily ensconced in the costume drama of life in Mumbai, surrounded by people wearing brilliant disguises designed to attract applause. The goals had been set early—we were cheered on to win the lemon-and-spoon race, score the best marks in school, land the right job, cultivate a personality, find a partner, acquire a home, a second home ... The list went on and on. And we would repeat the cycle on autopilot with our children.

I, too, had learnt to curate my life intelligently, with all the requisite masks and costumes. I went to the right schools and colleges. I had a rocking career as a journalist with *The Times of India* and was a published author; my adorable young son and I were cocooned amidst a warm extended family and had wonderful friends.

For various reasons, my husband—let's call him P—and I lived in separate homes after about ten years of marriage, though we never gave up on our friendship and love for each other. I carried on with life, putting on more masks, gathering awards and feeling fine. Mostly. But every so often, when I was alone, away from the chatter, I felt different. Gradually, grudgingly, I began to acknowledge that I was living with a chronic undertow of melancholy that lapped back and forth. It was like having a toothache that you learn to ignore, live with, and expertly camouflage. I was irritated that I had to learn how to pay bills online. I was overwhelmed by the responsibility of raising a child on my own. Most of all, I felt heartbroken. Alone.

I should have been happy, but I was not. I couldn't understand why my intellect and my emotions were misaligned, like twin sisters not on talking terms. It baffled me. My friends would exchange glances every time I spaced out mid-sentence, a wobbly coping mechanism for my almost-depression.

Basically, my life was not going according to plan. Wait, let me clarify that—it was not going according to *my* plan. I didn't know then that there might be a bigger masterplan.

At some point during our separation, P and I had decided to file for divorce. It was logical. It was amicable. But the thing about divorce is that no matter what the reason or who initiates it, it can be emotionally wrenching.

I braced myself for the day when we had to show up at the Family Court in a dystopian, treeless suburb of Mumbai. The court building's leprous walls and indifferent architecture offered little solace to the traumatised. Long waits and the absence of a decent canteen made it worse. But we stepped outside on to a broken pavement for chai and cigarettes, and managed to laugh at each other's jokes, pretending that nothing was going to change.

At one point, P turned his back to me to check a phone message, the beep a chime of disharmony between us. I knew then that, underneath the mirth, I was feeling deep despair, and that I would need my close friends to prop me up, so I sent out a few plaintive messages and quickly organised a 'divorce party' for later that evening.

It happened to be Karva Chauth that day. My best friend messaged to say that she would make it for the evening but would have to rush up to the terrace to look at the moon through a sieve. My friend was fasting for her husband's longevity, while I was closing the door on a ritual that I didn't even believe in. Besides, that day, I wanted my husband dead. I certainly did not want him to live long and enjoy himself while I did bus stop duty and attended couples' dinners solo. I suddenly felt enraged and hurt and a little fearful.

Our common divorce lawyer was irked with us because we had started the divorce proceedings some years back but never followed through. Finally, today, the case would be closed, and she could get her full fee. She sat patiently with us in the crowded waiting room filled with all kinds of people, while I distracted myself by making up imaginary stories about each one's reasons for breaking up. We eventually walked into the little courtroom where a judge—a tiny woman who wore her hair in a low bun—told us, 'Sorry, this divorce cannot happen right now.'

The judge had rejected the divorce on a technical point and that was that. We were surprised. Then we started laughing. The lawyer could not believe it—we were among the oddest clients she had represented, and she had seen her fair share of contentious fools battling over airline miles and overpriced art. The two of us didn't even seem to want the divorce. She shrugged, P shrugged, I shrugged, and we went our separate ways. But I didn't cancel my divorce-cum-Karva Chauth party. The paneer and prawns had already been made.

That day was a reality check. Clearly, not everything goes according to plan. Or, well, everything does go according to plan, but the universe's plan is way more incredible and intricate than our individual minds can fathom.

❧

Those years were difficult. My son C was young and vulnerable. There were days when I propped myself up to be present for him and to pre-empt my acute self-absorption from crushing us both. I felt sad every time he felt sad, or maybe he wasn't even sad and I was projecting my own sadness on to him. I don't know. Parenting is a strange game that comes with no manual.

I'll never forget these words that emerged from the child's mouth when he was six or seven: 'I happened because you and Papu came together, and now y'all are not together, so do I still exist?' I cannot remember what my garbled response was, but I do remember feeling a bolt of lacerating pain. Had I failed my child? Had I failed myself?

The perfect world that I had curated around me was not working the way I had thought it would. For a while, I felt like I was living the anxiety dream where you are endlessly late for an exam. I began to realise that I had to repair something within, not just rely on external circumstances and insidious reward systems. I started doing yoga regularly. I went for therapy. Tentatively, grudgingly, I turned to various self-help practices—all of which I had once smugly thought were not for me.

I didn't get to the point of picking tarot cards or meeting dodgy astrologers. The most out-of-character move I made at the time was going to a hypnotherapist, who tried her best to induce me to walk metaphorically down some stairs into the garden of my subconscious. Despite her expert efforts, I just couldn't travel 'down', let alone reach any greenery; it was all vaguely comical. She advised me to retreat for a while into nature to open and release the clutter that was blocking my interior road maps. I had to Marie Kondo my mind. That was the only way out.

I described my non-garden moment to a friend who worked on alternative healing modules. He went online and found me an Ayurvedic centre overlooking the vast and calming Mulshi Lake a few hours' drive from Mumbai. It was going to be my Walden Pond.

I went there for two weeks to detox mind and body, to stare at the water and meditate on falling leaves and do little else; doing is so often a distraction from being. It was the first time I was giving my brain a short sabbatical from its habitual egocentric excursions, going round and round without getting anywhere new. It was also the first time I was taking a different route, trusting something beyond the rational mind, something that would help me stop feeling low.

But nothing in life is random.

I did not know then that this lingering thread of sadness would become an inflection point. It sent me looking for answers. My melancholic state had been triggered by an external event but ended up scratching at the scab of an emptiness within that had perhaps always been there, always looking to be temporarily filled. I could no longer rely on the props that I had so carefully set up around me. One of them had collapsed, now the whole structure was teetering.

The slow burn of gloom helped me realise that my intellect or Ivy League education or wealth or relationships may not always help me control the outcomes. Sorrow, untimely death, the many confounding situations that contradict everything you assumed to be true—nothing I possessed helped me understand all this. Why do bad things happen to good people? Why do even highly successful people feel an emptiness, a sudden sense of terror? How is it that we all know that death is inevitable but live our lives as if it will never happen? What are those unseen factors that drive all things, including what some call coincidences and others call miracles? These are questions that people have been asking for millennia. Now, I too wanted some answers.

So, when my childhood friend Shona said, 'Namu, trust me, just come to Rishikesh,' I didn't overthink it. I took the flight to Dehradun's Jolly Grant airport, drove past dense forests and a dry riverbed, and found myself in a serene ashram on the banks of a roaring river, far away from the bustle of the town.

IN THE LAP OF THE HIMALAYAS

Rishikesh has long attracted sadhus, seekers, hippies and pilgrims. It spreads on both sides of the Ganga, where the river is still an icy blue before it heads across the plains and gathers in its swirls the detritus of human life.

Because of its location on India's Karma Cola map, the city has a faintly international vibe. Like a demigod in a mythological tele-serial, you can whoosh from a hipster café called German Bakery to an underground ashram that might engage in a secret practice of tantric yoga. Hinduism cannot be put into a box, especially here. It is available to all in its many versions, all of them acceptable.

The place is also steeped in stories and myths. If you cross the river via either of the two suspension bridges commemorating brotherly love, named Lakshman Jhula and Ram Jhula, you can watch a dazzling sound-and-light show customised for the spiritual Instagrammer. Then, there's the cave where a young monk once went into deep meditation seeking answers. It may not make it to even the footnote of a travel book, but the spot exudes an inexplicable energy, like smoke from a camphor stick, its fragrance lingering forever.

At some point, the irresistible combination of the river and the spiritual aura of the place attracted India's national predator, the real-estate shark. Some enterprising (undoubtedly pious) folks created an exclusive gated community of bungalows along the riverside. Some of these houses are now hemmed in by rows of newer structures, yet again illustrating the abiding Hindu idea that nothing is permanent, definitely not a river view.

But Rishikesh's languid energy can be beguiling. It is also the point from which thousands of pilgrims embark on the four-abodes pilgrimage—Yamunotri, Gangotri, Badrinath and Kedarnath—in search of the elusive ash-covered mountain god who wears Rudraksha seeds around his neck and calmly observes creation as well as devastation in all the universe. Eyes gently shut. In neutral silence.

I arrived at the ashram in December 2014, not knowing what to expect, trusting my girlfriend who had tasted the magic potion and wanted me to try it. I was as overwhelmed and as excited as when I walked into the Princeton University campus clutching two VIP suitcases many years ago. I was going to be a student again. Instead of ivy-covered gothic buildings and archways, I saw in front of me an enormous peepul tree, a temple and an aquamarine river.

In the 1960s, around the time the Beatles were learning transcendental meditation in Rishikesh, a young journalist called Natarajan from Tamil Nadu's Tiruvarur district, who had been studying Hindu philosophy, came here to meditate quietly on the knowledge he had acquired. He had been learning under Chinmayananda, a highly regarded scholar and teacher of Hinduism. But even after many years of rigorous study, something kept troubling him. The loop was not closing. So, with his teacher's blessings, he went to study further in a small town called Gudivada in Andhra Pradesh before finally arriving in Rishikesh. He came to a small grove of rosewood trees called sheeshamwadi, and built himself a hut by the river. This became home. Over the next few years, Natarajan withstood the extreme temperatures, bathed in the Ganga and stood in line with others to get food from unknown benefactors.

But a seeker must be patient, like Nandi the bull in repose. No one knows when the fruit will ripen. Sometimes, a musician may know all there is to know about a raga, and yet something is missing when she performs. Then, one day, a tabla accompanist might casually suggest that she pause a bit more on the madhyam note, and suddenly the music is transformed.

The young Natarajan's moment of understanding came while he was talking to a wandering ascetic. Who was this wise man who gave him this final key? It doesn't even matter. Wisdom is freely available to all those who pause to breathe it in. And there are many different paths to the same truth, which is always latent, awaiting discovery. Some emphasise the need to study scriptures. Others meditate in silence.

By and by, Natarajan became Swami Dayananda Saraswati (not to be confused with the founder of the

Arya Samaj), a teacher whose brilliance and affable, non-judgemental nature attracted more and more students to him from all over the country. A school of spiritual education came up, with teaching halls and dormitories, establishing itself amidst many other centres of learning and contemplation in Rishikesh. Using the scriptures as his base, this erudite scholar eventually created a curriculum for a rigorous three-year programme that was designed to equip many more to teach and interpret—almost a PhD in philosophy and faith. It was into this lineage of teaching that I had landed.

One of Dayananda Saraswati's students was Neema Majmudar, an economist by training, who quit her profession to become a teacher of Hindu philosophy. She moved from Bangkok to Mumbai to teach what she had learnt, continuing an age-old guru-shishya tradition: the master teaches a student and the student then evolves into a master. Her husband Surya, also a follower of the same tradition, was teaching management students how to apply this wisdom to the study of contemporary business practices. Every year, Neema and Surya held an immersive retreat in this ashram by the river.

Neema was quite unlike my idea of a spiritual teacher. She seemed as comfortable sipping wine as she was chanting Vedic mantras. I didn't know it then, but Neema was going to be the unusual white rabbit I followed into a new wonderland.

The ashram in Rishikesh was where I first encountered the Upanishads and the Bhagavad Gita, ancient texts that I had been only vaguely familiar with in my almost-fifty years on this planet. It was a ten-day course, and I made it for the second half, partly because this was such new territory that I wanted to dip my toe in before attempting to swim, and partly because I didn't like being away from my fifteen-year-old son for very long.

The rooms in the ashram were simple and spare, almost austere. There was no heating. We had to wash our plates and cutlery with freezing cold water in a large communal sink outside the dining hall. There was no question of stepping out for a cigarette, and the entire city was alcohol-free. I commended myself for at least moving out of my comfort zone and trying something new. But I was tentative, suspicious of a space and a language so unlike anything I knew. I was also a little weirded out about turning into someone I may not recognise, or even particularly like. I was scared that my former self might scoff at my current self, embarrassed that my friends would think I had turned right-wing or joined some creepy cult. For the longest time, I had sneered at the idea of Vedic ashrams, sanyasis in tangerine-coloured robes and temples where you could buy your way into the fast-track queue to god. Faith was a very private affair; I prayed transactionally, asking for this or that, and occasionally with gratitude, thanking some god for some good that had happened.

But life takes you where you are meant to go. I was about to unearth, like an accidental archaeologist, a spiritual map of India, populated by those who were unbothered by the chatter of opinion or the banality of judgement. Many of those I encountered along the way were brilliant thinkers and teachers. There were some who were wise and saintly, also some who were wily charlatans. But most were folks who had decided to take an excursion into unchartered terrain: the journey within. They were homeward bound.

Every year, during the retreat, Neema taught a selection of verses from a particular Upanishad, along with verses from the Bhagavad Gita that complement them. The Upanishads and the Gita essentially reveal the same truth, but come to it from different perspectives, one more abstract, the other placed within a very human story set on the battlefield of Kurukshetra. This year, she had picked verses from the Chandogya Upanishad, which starts as a dialogue between a father and son. The father, Uddalaka, speaks to his son, Svetaketu, about dependent and absolute reality, and how to differentiate between the two. He uses the example of a clay pot to show that oneness is the underlying truth of our existence. Pots may be of different shapes and sizes, but they are all made of clay. The pots cannot exist without clay, but the clay exists independent of the form. Similarly, a gold ornament has a particular form, say as a bangle or a necklace, but it comes from gold and goes back into gold when melted down. We are all forms taking different shapes at different times, but our essence is the same.

The idea was not new to me, but it was being recast and presented in an irrefutably logical way. I had encountered a similar concept in the troubadour saint Kabir's marvellously counter-intuitive poetry: we are all mud, taking on different forms. These forms are what we take to be real, but from mud we come and into mud we return. Whether made from humble clay or precious gold, however different in shape or beauty, the underlying truth is essentially the same. Clay and gold, Neema said to us, are like the substratum that we call Brahmn or abiding consciousness.

It made sense, and it didn't make sense. Our teacher assured us that these ideas were so audacious and so contrary to the way we had been conditioned to think that it would take a while for them to percolate, even longer to sink in. Which is why the first stage, shravana, or repetitive listening, is such a big part of learning, to help ease out prior concepts and create a new mental infrastructure.

I had heard these ideas before, but this time I was transfixed, despite some confusion and many questions. Perhaps you need your world to be shaken up to really accept the idea that we all come from one place and return to the same place, and that oneness is the underlying truth of our existence. We have grown so used to labelling people—this one is Hindu or Muslim or Sikh or Christian; went to X college; lives in Y neighbourhood; is clever/dumb; is beautiful/ugly; is black/brown/white. It's all right to use descriptors, as long as they are describing the difference between, say, a red hibiscus and a yellow rose. But is one better than the other? No. Different? Yes. Subjectivity can be enormously liberating, but preferences and prejudices are meaningless beyond a point. Eventually, the pink rose, the ugly person and the clever one will all resolve into one singular unifying whole, call it clay or gold. Or death.

As she sat in front of us, day after day, in a hall filled with the sincerest group of students, she explained each concept with such clarity that it started making some sense.

'Imagine a limitless expanse of space, above and below, in front of you and behind you, to the right and the left. Basically, everywhere,' she said.

She picked up a glass and held it up.

'Now, in this space is placed this glass. Automatically, it is filled with the same space. There is space inside the glass as well as outside, but the glass defines a particular confined space, correct?' She looked around at the many blank faces before her, each of us trying to absorb this non-physics experiment and explanation.

'You are the space that is both contained inside the glass, and the space that continues to exist, whether or not the glass is there. The glass is the form that your body has taken, but the space remains even after the glass is broken.'

We studied for several hours in the day, and then, in keeping with Neema's belief that the scriptures should never keep one from having fun, we went shawl shopping or gathered in a little tea shop called Gayatri just outside the ashram gates. The students, who had come from different parts of India and the world, were a diverse bunch—a Frenchman who headed a luxury brand in Paris, a Mumbai executive who worked in private equity, a German couple who ran a yoga studio in their Bavarian village, a psychiatrist from Thane who was able to connect the workings of the brain with spirituality. A hilarious Israeli man made up a funny song about the proverbial clay pots and why we must marry early while the clay is still malleable. A sand artist from Berlin, who had been studying Hindu scriptures for several years, declared, 'Namita, you are so lucky to be from this land, but we usually take for granted what is right under our nose.'

I remember that moment when my constructed, conditioned versions of 'self' started dissolving, the disguises started peeling off.

It was the last morning of the retreat, which also happened to be my forty-seventh birthday. The previous evening, I had been sitting on a bench facing the river and the hill on the other side of it. I could see the cave where George Harrison had once hung out with Maharshi Mahesh Yogi. A quiet mist ascended from the water and I felt my eyes tearing. It may have been from sadness or joy, or both, or neither. The aquamarine water and the emerald green hill in the distance turned into Impressionist art in my blurred vision. I blinked a few times and saw a speck of tangerine in the distance. As it came closer, the object morphed into a monk.

Then, the bells started to chime. First one, and then many, in symphonic unison, little and big bells that hung at the entrances of temples all around, until they reached a crescendo, distant but also simultaneously vibrating within me.

I remembered what a qawwali singer at Ajmer Sharif had once told me: Music is always an offering in temples and churches and mausoleums.

'This is why you find a bell at the entrance in places of worship. And this is why we sing in the dargah or in a gurudwara,' he said, pausing to engage with his spittoon. 'Even when a dacoit is about to attack someone, and he hears a temple bell, he will involuntarily stop in his tracks, even if only for a moment. This is kachcha jadoo, primordial magic.' And back he went to his music, belting out more boisterous Allahoos.

It felt like I was in a timeless space. I could have been sitting there centuries ago, or at some point in the future. It didn't really matter. Our version of the 'self' is as ephemeral as the clothes we wear and discard. We are all clay, mutable, and therefore capable of what psychologists call neuroplasticity: the human being's in-herent potential to transform into anything they wish to be. A rogue bandit can become a saint; a warrior king could become a Buddhist monk.

I was ready. Early the next morning, I took my first plunge in the icy water, with my teachers Neema and Surya on either side, ready to support me if I slipped on the rocks. But I didn't fall. After a few minutes, the cold didn't matter either. I felt exhilarated as I dunked my head underwater. I looked up at the rising sun, in the comforting company of strangers, breathing in the heady oxygen of faith. The people around me did this every morning, taking a dip as though it was just a part of the day's routine, as normal as packing your child's lunch box. I had tears in my eyes, from the cold and the feeling that accompanies a willing surrender of the will. I folded my hands. Shivering, I whispered the Gayatri mantra while facing the sun. That golden ball rising in the distance was not merely a star that unfailingly and unconditionally lit up the world, but also a symbol of illumination that erased the darkness of ignorance.

I remember there was a plump black bird sitting on a rock in the middle of the river, just sitting there, and I had this spontaneous thought that maybe this fat, feathered creature was my beloved grandmother, who had come to bless me. I cannot believe I am even sharing something so fanciful, but I think at that moment I wanted to suspend reason and break down the ideas and ideologies that had for so long governed my thoughts and emotions. So, for those few minutes, I allowed the bird to become my Dadi and send me her ghee-filled blessings from some Punjabi heaven.

As I climbed up the stone steps, dripping wet, ecstatic, I noticed a cluster of little statues on a ledge alongside the steps. A white marble Nandi, several black stone Shiva lingams, an abstract Ganesha with just the suggestion of a trunk folding out of the stone. Ambrosial, organic art. Fresh golden-yellow marigolds were sprinkled around them and aromatic sandalwood smoke snaked out of an incense stick. Who had lit it? Who had created this priest-less temple without any boundary walls? A peacock feather lay on the step above. I gingerly picked it up and stepped into the first day of the rest of my life.

There is something very liberating about letting go of long-held concepts and handing over your power of attorney to a greater, even if unfathomable, force. Looking back, I wonder if I was dissolving the barriers of manifest forms, of past and present, of waking and dreaming, of life and death, and life again. Around me, so many others seemed to be living their lives based on this kind of surrender, what many patronisingly describe as 'faith'.

Faith is underrated.

The saint Ramakrishna Paramahamsa writes: 'First realise God, then think of creation and the world. If you know one, you know all. If you put fifty zeros after a one, you have a large sum but erase the one and nothing remains.'

Consider also this instance of faith: when Ravana, the villain in the Ramayana epic, was trying to win Sita over, his friends said to him, 'To court Sita's favour you took on so many different disguises, why don't you now go to her in the guise of Rama?' He replied, 'When I contemplate on Rama, I cannot even imagine seeking out another man's wife.'

I view faith as that plane beyond the binaries of good and bad, moral and immoral. Just as a blade of grass in the gusty wind bends but does not break, relinquishing control can give you strength. The twelve-step programme started by Alcoholics Anonymous is based on the edifying recognition that you may have very little control over your compulsions. At some point you surrender to a 'higher power' and ask for help.

I remember chatting with a friend of C's who was studying in Canada and was home for the holidays. He was describing a violent snowstorm that had debilitated parts of North America and delayed flights. The flight home was so turbulent that the stewardess spontaneously announced: 'Stay calm and pray.' The child said, 'I remembered every Parsi prayer I had ever been taught and just kept muttering them until we landed!'

Although I desisted from blurting an aunty-ish comment, I thought to myself, 'Why wait for bad weather? Pray for a few minutes every day, as a kind of pause, just as you would brush your teeth. If you can't think of what to ask for, ask simply to be in alignment with the higher order of the universe.'

So, that year, I had my first dip in the river and my first introduction to a body of knowledge that was different from anything I had ever encountered. I learnt that nothing is random. There's a plan in place, you just have to decode the signs—if you choose to. And if you don't, that's also fine, but it might mean getting tossed around in the turbulence some more.

I feel humans are like the stones that a river brings down from the mountains. Some stones keep journeying on; they remain rough and get pushed around; some break down into fertile soil along the banks, nourishing plant and animal life. And some get polished and smoothened over centuries. Then, one day, a passerby might pick up the smooth stone, anoint it with a smear of tangerine, and turn it into her god of small things.

Water, the ocean especially, has often been used as a metaphor to describe that infinite consciousness from which everything comes and into which everything goes: the basis of Hindu Vedic philosophy. I have noticed that, alongside almost every place of worship in India is a water body. Is it there to remind us of the infinite?

Water is also a reminder of who we are: nearly 70 per cent of the human body is water. We are a part of nature, not outside it. When we lose touch with nature, we lose touch with ourselves. Everything—the tides, the banyan trees, a feather, a sunbeam—is connected to who we are and is teaching us something.

Water does not increase or decrease, it changes form. Answers float in the circularity of water, in how it evaporates into clouds from which rain falls to fill water bodies that find their way back into the ocean. A river is constantly in flux; you never step into the same one twice. It circumvents obstacles, benefits many along the way and eventually finds its way home, turning saline just before it enters the sea.

I suspect that human beings also long to be in harmony with themselves and with that ocean of the infinite, even if we are not necessarily aware of this. Everyone is seeking the same answers, searching for freedom from sadness or a sense of smallness. But most of us seek it in the perceptible material world, in relationships, or money and fame, or even spiritual entertainment. And yet, even after we achieve whatever it is we set out to do, we feel a restlessness for something bigger, more permanent and unshakeable. Intuitively, I knew I had to sink my feet deeper into these white sand banks.

My relationship with the Ganga began rather hilariously. I was heavily pregnant and working at *The Times of India* when my boss called me to his office and whispered conspiratorially: 'Namita, I am sending you on a secret mission. Madonna is in Banaras. Go find her and do the story. Keep it hush-hush. It's a big scoop.'

Armed with this information alone, I hopped on to a flight and landed up in the world's oldest living city, also known as Kashi, the city of Shiva. Like Rishikesh, Banaras has a seductive other-worldly quality, a kind of ambient ancientness that touches anyone who enters its precincts. This reveals itself in the lilt of ordinary conversations filled with poetry and philosophy, and lies buried in the stone steps or ghats that border the river. India's greatest musicians have lived and performed here. Bismillah Khan used to speak whimsically about the river being a part of his home and how the god Shiva came to him and sprayed him with attar. And when Chhannulal Mishra sings the Ramcharitmanas, you can hear the flavour of a Banarasi paan in his voice. In Banaras, life and death are given equal footage; I read somewhere that one arrives with a full-blown ego and leaves as a speck of ash.

On that assignment, soon after I reached, I literally started walking around the ghats, asking random locals whether they might know if a blonde American pop singer was staying in one of the ashrams. Though armed with the thick skin of an inquisitive journalist, I still felt a bit loony. Then someone pointed me to a canary-yellow low-rise. At the end of a vast courtyard, a middle-aged man sat cross-legged on a velvet sofa the colour of betel juice. He was a Sanskrit teacher. Let's call him Tiwariji. I asked him if Madonna was at his ashram. He scratched his belly, smiled beatifically and nodded sagely, but said nothing. I couldn't tell whether he was protecting her privacy or had no clue what I was babbling about. Or maybe he was stoned. I left a short while after his student informed me that he was on an indefinite silent fast.

Later that day, while sitting in a café (which had a Hebrew menu alongside the English one), I met a local reporter, Ishana, who said he would meet me the following day and give me the scoop on Madonna. 'But I cannot tell you exactly what time, as I only live in the present moment.' Ishana was only half joking. I was beginning to realise that Banaras was a city of mad hatters.

Here's what I found out. Madonna had released a terrible song called '*Shanti Ashtangi*' in which she had sung some lines in Sanskrit. Ishana played it for his pal, the silent Tiwariji, who casually remarked that her pronunciation was completely off. Like a good journalist who can conjure up a story out of vapour to fulfil his weekly quota, Ishana filed a piece for a wire service: 'Sanskrit scholar says Madonna song all wrong'. The piece went out and was picked up by BBC Radio, which then decided to do a call-in with Madonna and the Sanskrit teacher, with Ishana as interlocuter. This was how Madonna had 'reached' Banaras. Somehow the myth started circulating, gathering colour along the way, that Madonna was learning Sanskrit from Tiwariji, and he clearly did not feel obliged to correct the story. Tiwariji was one of many who had set up shop in the great Indian spiritual marketplace. He was both learned and street smart, a scholar as much as a trickster, like a beguiling Banarasi textile that weaves together two differently coloured threads.

But my scoop had just been cremated.

Tired and despondent, I retreated to my host's house, preparing to find my way back to the office and face a disappointed boss. But Banaras, the city of magic realism, has its own version of prasada for those who seek. I was staying with a relative who taught ecology at Banaras Hindu University. Seeing that I was feeling sorry for myself, she sent me to meet her colleague, a man called Veerbhadra Mishra.

I soon discovered why. This elegant, elderly scholar was a professor of hydraulic engineering and also the hereditary priest of the Sankat Mochan Temple that housed the monkey warrior god, Hanuman. Veerbhadra Mishra was an environmentalist and a devotee in equal measure. For him, the river was not merely a water body but a divine presence, and he was committed to cleaning it. Behind the temple, on Tulsi Ghat, he had set up a chemistry lab where he daily monitored the bacteria levels in the Ganga.

Veerbhadra Mishra defied any arguments that suggest a rift between faith and reason, mysticism and the material world. He believed, like many scientists had before him, that the two can align to offer a far richer, more meaningful understanding of the universe. At one point, there was a proposal to start an electric crematorium on the ghats so that half-burned bodies wouldn't further pollute the river, and he used his position as temple head to support it.

When I met him, he was sitting erect on his bed, in front of a picture window that framed the river beyond. He talked about many things, including how Hanuman's devotion was the secret behind his supernatural powers, and how we all have that same potential. He spoke about Shiva, the presiding deity of Banaras, and why the abstract shape of the lingam that represents the god is both form and formlessness, encompassing all there is to know about the universe.

Veerbhadra Mishra spoke about the Ganga with the deepest love, as if it were a family elder, not a geographical entity. He said that our bodies are a microcosm of the planet and are made up of the same elements—earth, wind, space, water, fire. So, when we pollute the earth, we are polluting ourselves.

I had read about how even insentient beings like trees and rivers have an intelligence the human mind cannot fathom. How else do trees talk to each other and share nutrients through underground networks? And how do migratory birds move across continents without Google Maps to guide them?

How does a river always find its way to the ocean?

'Don't think of stones as dead objects. Write Rama's name on them and they will form a bridge over oceans,' Mishra said. 'Faith can change everything.'

As the light over the river started changing, I could see a boat downstream flickering like a firefly. Or maybe it was a lamp carrying someone's prayer. A tendril of smoke rose from the opposite bank, vanishing into the darkness. Veerbhadra Mishra took me to his lab where many test tubes with differing levels of water in them stood in a line, awaiting examination; after that, to the temple where he chanted evening prayers for the son of the wind. It was an improbable, perfect place. And I got my story.

BRAHMN

Brahmn is a term in Vedic thought that will recur in this story I'm trying to tell, so I am going to attempt to explain it, even if it is indescribable. Certainly, it cannot be comprehended by the intellect. It is an idea beyond vocabulary, but because we use language as the means to make sense of most things, let us call it 'consciousness'.

The root of Brahmn in Sanskrit is Brh, which means 'big'—and it's a noun, not an adjective.

Brahmn is not to be confused with Brahma, the creator. Nor with the Brahmin caste.

Brahmn is the substratum of everything. It is that vast unchanging ocean of awareness that remains unruffled by individual drama. It has no attributes. It is where we come from, what we are, and what we resolve into—even as we occupy individual bodies and minds—of a Namita or a tree or a rock or a song. Everything happens within Brahmn. It is the only thing that is real, independent and infinite. All else—our lives, our glories, our despair—is transient and, therefore, not real. Is this what Buddhists call Shunya?

Listen to the unstruck note ... to the roar of silence ... to that which is beyond words ... to that which is beyond the beyond.

❧

Close both eyes
To see with the other eye

*– Rumi**

* *Rumi Poems*, edited by Peter Washington and published by Alfred A. Knopf, 2006.

BRAHMACHARYA

THE ACCIDENTAL STUDENT

There have always been within me two divergent tracks jostling to coexist: a longing for an ancientness and gratitude for all that modernity brings. This has been both confounding and comforting. For the longest time, I used to feel a dissonance, a sense of unbelonging, until the tracks became parallel. Then I saw that both are needed for the train to move smoothly.

This is the story of those early days and some of my teachers, including a very tall man with a pocket watch, a grandaunt who played Chaupad and a beloved music teacher.

THE SECRET LIBRARY

My childhood unfolded slowly, like a black-and-white Doordarshan film on a Sunday evening. It was easy and predictable, with the occasional vague anxiety of unfinished homework. I grew up in socialist India. We entertained ourselves by playing hide-and-seek with other children in the building and reading Amar Chitra Katha comics, which took us through the looking glass into a land of gods and demons who could turn humans into swans ...

On the weekends, we went with family friends to Borivli National Park where we ate melty potatoes with round-round puris, rejoicing when Coca-Cola arrived in India and brought fizz to the picnic. Or we went to a hill-station farm in Lonavala, where we watched our grandfather milk buffaloes named Phoolan and Gopi, and gagged when handed stainless steel glasses of smelly milk with yellowish cream floating on top. When we drove back down the Western Ghats, we would stay awake until we came to a little temple under a peepul tree and stopped to receive pieces of dry coconut wrapped in scraps of newspaper. We would munch on them and fall asleep, dreaming of Noddy and

Narasimha, and a demoness called Hidimbi who married a handsome prince called Bheema.

I must have been about ten when my parents invited a retired professor from Allahabad, called Dayashankar Dubey, to read Hindi literature to my sister and me. This tall, gentle figure would arrive at our door on Saturday mornings in his beige hand-spun kurta, white dhoti and Gandhi cap, smelling faintly of clove or something else pungent and unfamiliar. His only mandate was to introduce us to Hindi stories, Sanskrit poetry, the epics, so that we could marinate in their lyrical wisdom. We called him Masterji.

'Ram Ram Masterji,' we would chortle.

'Ram Ram,' he would reply, and once again at my sister, 'Ram Ram bitiya'... See, because there are two of you, I get to invoke Ram twice!'

He would set his cane down, take off his cap, and sit at our dining table while my sister and I stood fidgeting, already anticipating boredom. He would take off his eyeglasses, dab the film of perspiration on his face, and then wipe the almost opaque glass with a handkerchief, making it clear he did not care for urgency. He did not wear a wristwatch; instead, in his breast pocket he carried a small old-fashioned steel watch that he sometimes pulled out. After having his first sip of tea, he would ask whether we wanted to listen to the dramatic story of Karna or read a story by Rabindranath Tagore, calmly ignoring the insouciance with which we responded to his mention of these pearls.

'Come, recite the verses I had told you to learn by heart,' he would say, turning to me, knowing that I had probably spent my spare time reading an Archie comic instead. Veronica versus Saraswati.

Rather than admonish me, he would recite the verses slowly with me, gently correcting my pronunciation or explaining the meaning of 'shweta padmasana', a sartorial description of the goddess of scholarship. He made us write the lines down in our lined notebooks, for he said writing helped memorisation. He urged us to turn our Hindi handwriting into 'little gems laid in a neat line across the page'.

Some days, Masterji told us stories about the saintly teachers of India. I vividly remember someone called Nisargadatta because of one unusual detail—he made beedis for a living in a tiny room in the heart of old Bombay. To us, he didn't sound like a serene sage, for Masterji had told us how he would speak in crude Marathi, swearing and shouting at the students who would assemble hungrily in front of him.

'But he had the key to the treasure. Never judge someone by their external appearance, children.'

One day, Masterji made us read a poem by someone called Ralph Waldo Emerson and told us that he was an American philosopher and poet who had been moved by the Bhagavad Gita.

'But wasn't he a Christian?' I protested, being of an age that precedes nuance.

'You do not have to be Hindu to follow Hinduism,' he said. 'Now, don't you learn physics laws discovered by Newton and Galileo? They were also rishis—rishis of science. Knowledge does not have any geography. All rivers and streams eventually reach the same ocean. This is where everyone has gone all wrong, the priests, the devotees, all. What do you think is the purpose of religion?' He seemed to be looking at something distant, momentarily distracted, before quickly dissolving back into the present.

Masterji then seamlessly recited a line from the Ramcharitmanas, in which Ram tells his brother Lakshman:

Par hita saris dharam nahin bhai,
Par peeda sam nahin athmai ...

There is no greater religion than doing good for others,
and there is no worse sin than harming others.

Masterji was the first liberal intellectual in my life, one deeply entrenched in his faith but equally respectful of all believers, including atheists. He introduced us to the poetry of Kabir. We learnt from him that no one knew if Kabir was a Hindu or a Muslim. The son of a weaver, he turned all certainties on their head, engaging with the warp and weft of life's mysterious ways.

Bura jo dekhan mei chalaa, bura na miliya koye
Jo man dekha aapana, mujhse bura na koye

I set out to look for bad in others, but didn't find it,
When I looked within, I realised that there was none worse than me.

This was agenda-less learning. There were no tests, no competitive exams. It was my parents' noble intervention to supplement our Anglophone education, a model that had been masterfully designed to kick anything 'vernacular' to a lower rung. It was also about getting us to absorb the cadence of Hindi, expand our vocabulary in a language that was gradually fading out of our lives.

A villager may be able to recite the entire Ramcharitmanas or sing the poetry of Tukaram, but among a certain English-speaking elite, he would likely be considered quaint and primitive rather than literary. For we were busy drinking water from Italian blown glass even if earthen cups were the more hygienic, eco-friendly and, to my eyes, aesthetically superior option.

One day, in the month of December, Masterji was in the middle of telling us a story about a ruthless forest bandit called Ratnakar when the phone rang. It was the old land line instrument. Bhakti Maya, our beloved helper who raised us, answered it and then grinned her toothless grin. 'Baby hua.'

My grandmother had called from the hospital to tell us that our baby sister had just bounced into the world. Instantly, we both bolted out of our chairs and started jumping on the sofa and whooping, for we had just been given our biggest toy. Bhakti Maya was dabbing her eyes—I am still uncertain whether from joy or regret that it was yet another girl.

'Now that Lakshmi has arrived, there is no way you are going to concentrate on anything I say,' said Masterji with a laugh, picking up his walking stick.

A few weeks later, his nephew called to say that Masterji had passed on peacefully in his sleep. So, it was a long while before we found out that the forest bandit eventually became Valmiki and wrote a brilliant epic called Ramayana, which would give us that life-affirming insight: everyone—even a cruel dacoit—has the potential to transform.

Ashes to ashes, dust to dust. At the age of twelve, I had no idea how to cope with death. I remember feeling blank. I missed Masterji's presence and remorsefully learnt the entire Saraswati shloka and a couplet by Kabir in remembrance of him.

Maati kahe kumbhar se, tu kya rondhe mohe
Ek din aisa aayega, main rondhungi tohe…

The mud tells the potter, don't think you can
knead and shape me forever.
The day will come when I will be doing the same
thing to you.

Simple, irrefutable, levelling wisdom that should pop up as a weekly reminder for each one of us, along with gold prices and weather forecasts.

If the red slayer think he slays,
Or if the slain think he is slain,
They know not well the subtle ways
I keep, and pass, and turn again.

*– Ralph Waldo Emerson**

---

* From Ralph Waldo Emerson's poem 'Brahma' (www.poetryfoundation.org).

THE PAST IS PRESENT

I have long had a blue statue of Rama in my living room. It is mostly decorative but, like the many subliminal narratives that drive us, I think I was drawn to it because the Prince of Ayodhya was such an ambient presence in my childhood.

In my paternal grandparents' home in Mumbai, we greeted each other with 'Ram Ram' and, so many years later, my cousins and I still begin our WhatsApp messages with RR, perhaps trying to evoke those summer vacations filled with pillow fights, Alphonso mangoes and an angry young Amitabh Bachchan towering high in a single-screen cinema hall.

In my mother's family, the standard greeting was 'Jai Ram Ji Ki'. As children, we sat cross-legged for hours stringing parijat flowers for our grandmother's idols, tongues sticking out in concentration to ensure we didn't pierce the delicate orange stems. During the Dussehra holidays, we went to watch the Ramleela in Delhi, in which Ram was played by a young actor called Bhushan; he was later replaced by a younger, equally talented, Rocky. The music and movements were adapted from the classical arts. Ravana leapt around wearing a Kathakali mask, his face twitching maniacally—sheer joy for us as kids. We were wonderstruck, never bored.

And when the triumphant trio and their devoted monkey warrior eventually returned to Ayodhya, we would gasp as the actors danced holding flickering lamps that never went out.

Afterwards, my cousins and I imitated Ravana or renamed each other Mandodari and Surpanakha and giggled for hours, concocting respite from the casual dysfunctionalities of our parents. Often, we would stretch out on a vast bed eating dahi samosas with our grand-aunt, Mausiji, while a thread of early winter crept in through the window, making us huddle closer under our soft cotton blankets.

Mausiji was like a magic storytelling box that could release silken thread after thread and wrap you in an endless reel. She told us that Rama was a noble man who exercised his choices judiciously. He didn't have to go away on exile but went graciously, advising his younger brother Bharata to look after the people of the kingdom while he took care of the beasts in the forest. He ate berries that had been tasted by another. He loved his wife enough to call for war.

'All the characters and events are instruments that enable a story to move a certain way,' said Mausiji, while laying out her Chaupad board on the bed. Flattening the four corners of the frayed textile cross that had been her long-time companion, she continued, 'Kaikeyi had to be the mean queen who ordered Rama's exile because she was part of a larger story that had to play out.'

'Everything happens in an orchestrated series of movements, for what is meant to be will be,' Mausiji said mysteriously, chuckling because she had long ago penetrated other realms and dreamt a particular dream that had changed her family's financial destiny.

As children, we could not fully comprehend what she meant, but her storytelling was the mother's milk that nourished us, especially when our emotional immunity was down.

'And what about making Sita go through the fire test in front of everyone?' I asked her.

'Valmiki's original Ramayana was different. In it, Rama drowns himself in sorrow,' she said. 'Besides, it was a different time, child. The king's public role was more important than his personal relationships. Rama may have been a god, but, in that moment in time, he was also human.'

But Rama was no ordinary human. He was compassionate even with his enemy. When Ravana collapsed with exhaustion on the battlefield on the first day, Rama advised him to go home and rest. When Ravana finally died, Rama asked his brother Vibhishana to perform the funeral rites with dignity and grace.

It was never personal.

We would sit around Mausiji, innocent Chaupad players without any motivation to load our dice with deceit. We veered between listening awestruck and dozing off while she recited the metred rhymes of the Ramcharitmanas from memory. Even now, I think of the jaunty Lakshmana and the devoted Hanuman with regard and a blur of cousinly love.

For years, until he became less pliable, I would take C to watch the Ramleela in Delhi because I wanted those epic emotions to colour his imagination and because he grew up greeting his grandparents with an anodyne 'Hi'.

And because the past is always present.

We are never without a context. We move forward in life using a system of internal navigation informed by our personal and collective histories. Everyone has a backstory that emerges from childhood, even going back to the womb. Further back is the generational debris that calcifies to block many psychological arteries. But we rarely commit to getting an angioplasty of our deeper selves. We continue to behave in irrational ways, stumbling through life, hurting others and ourselves along the way.

'The Freudian unconscious is a kind of scrap basket of repressed experiences that you can't tolerate. That you don't know how to assimilate ... it's a function of what you experience even before you knew you were experiencing it,' writes Joseph Campbell, the great mythologist, who studied the undercurrents in Hindu myths and suggested that the bizarre stories they held touched on those parts that lived well beyond the rational mind.

Of late, I have been thinking of the many ways in which the past shapes the self, not only the personal self, but a more intangible cultural and spiritual self that makes one think and behave in a very particular way: why I still prefer eating with my hands; how I greet my elders or don't touch a book with my feet; why I might pray to a stone or a tree; why I pray at all. It is a recognition of this continuity that drives my quest to connect with those fragments of our collective past that continue to influence us in subtle yet significant ways. It is an exploration that makes me feel more whole, somehow.

Jawaharlal Nehru described India as 'an ancient palimpsest on which layer upon layer of thought and reverie had been subscribed, and yet no succeeding layer had completely hidden or erased what had been written previously.' I imagine India as a digital hologram, of geography, clothes, music and faith, where some things stay, some change, all with a quiet confidence. Like the innovative vendor in Chennai who invented a 'bestseller sari' by stitching on a pocket at just the right place, before the pleats begin, to accommodate a mobile phone. It is a privilege to belong to a land with such complex layers and textures, where the old still casually coexists with the new, with steeples, minarets and temples all reaching for the same sky.

My understanding is that ancient India has an amorphous cultural base, from an early animism that bowed to the sun and the sky, to a later codified Vedic practice. Buddhism, Jainism and Sikhism grew out of this, repurposing many ideas to counter the stultification that had crept into what we could broadly describe as Hinduism, mutating its essence. Islam's contribution to the palimpsest has been magnificent, especially in the arts, architecture, language and food. Later, Christianity and the double-edged sword of colonialism gave us the English language.

I find it charming that we live in the midst of a multicultural history, rather than boxing things and sending them to a museum. I remember driving through coastal Maharashtra and discovering a fourteenth-century Portuguese fort and church, on the stone walls of which villagers were blithely spreading red chillies to dry. Near the chapel lay stone blocks with Latin engravings. My friend who lived near there joked that he had often considered casually picking up one of those pieces, but he never did because he knew that it would be inauspicious.

The cultural life of India is geared towards the human being's inner evolution. It is based on the belief that the material and the spiritual are intertwined. I marvel at how an intangible philosophy is braided into our customs and aesthetics so seamlessly. All around us, art, architecture, music have been coded with a network of ideas that you absorb without even knowing it. The lotus that you find in the pichhwai or in Buddhist art is not just pastoral imagery. It is a reminder to live in the mud of the material world and still bloom with transcendence, a detached attachment. In fact, you need the mud for the lotus to blossom. No mud, no lotus. The traditionally constructed temple symbolises the human form and its aspirations. The outer walls may have friezes depicting explicit sexual positions, but the inside is a quiet, stark space. The shikhara or steeple is eternally aspiring for something far beyond. The shrine is deep within the temple, in a place of darkness that lights up only during prayers, when the priest circles a flickering lamp around the idol.

I remember being drawn to the intriguing title of a talk by the late art historian B.N. Goswamy, 'The things we don't see'. During the talk, he showed us painting after painting, revealing what happens when we pause and look beyond what our eyes first beheld. He finally came to a painting of a tree shedding white flowers. He invited us to observe it more carefully. We gasped. For the white flowers were not drifting down randomly as we had initially thought. They had been carefully placed to invoke the form of Krishna. It was magic, and equally a lesson in pausing, looking beyond the immediate, connecting the dots—literally—to get to hidden truths. Such a pause also requires a surrender of that part of the ego which claims to know everything.

The purpose of art, architecture, music, is to elicit the 'aah' moment of bliss, beyond the 'waah' of praise. The writer Nabokov invokes this idea beautifully in his story, 'Music', in which a recently divorced couple find themselves in the same concert hall listening to an ethereal piece of music which, for that short time, cocoons them in an invisible dome of togetherness and eases their pain. Music can do that to you every so often. That evanescent feeling, transcending thought, rising above separateness, has been called ananda or bliss which, the sages say, is our true nature, sheathed by the drama of life.

Sat. Chit. Ananda.

Truth. Consciousness. Bliss.

Mausiji is blind. Masterji is long gone. And with them is gone whatever little access I had to Hindu literature and the epics. I went to an English-medium school and, besides, long after the British had left India, we were still colonising parts of ourselves so assiduously that it made us apologetic about our own culture.

So, I had not the faintest idea what the Hindu religious books contained. What on earth was an Upanishad? What was the Ashtavakra Gita, and how was it different from the Bhagavad Gita? In my world, the ancient scriptures were often viewed as religious (therefore the opposite of rational) rather than read for their literary merit or philosophical brilliance. What a loss—for they remain as relevant as they were thousands of years ago. The human condition never really changes, does it?

Over the years, words like 'moksha' and 'vedanta' have become ubiquitous yet elusive, usually showing up as brand names for spas or ethnic labels. Why would anyone bother chasing immortality when there are so many better things to seek—like partners and careers and money? I, too, had grown up viewing religion as either a primitive engagement or a political weapon. This was the first time that I found myself wanting to go beyond my biases, sift through the distortions, challenge my own superficial understanding that had been obscured by ritualistic practices and politics.

Being a bit of a nerd, I was not satisfied with the spiritual sound bites that were being freely dispensed by the new-age gurus who had popped up everywhere. I had to get to the source. My teacher Neema's spiritual lineage holds that the scriptures are a means of knowledge, and contain wisdom that you cannot reach through your senses and intellect. You need to study the texts to understand this knowledge with its diaphanous nuances. This was the same idea that my music teacher Dhondutai proclaimed—learn the precise grammar of the raga. Once you have the fundamentals in place, you can soar.

After my first dip in the Ganga, I started delving into the library of Hindu literature. I learnt of their perennial relevance and their ability to resonate with the human spirit, regardless of cultural or religious backgrounds. Here is a brief summary for those who may be as clueless as I was.

Vedas, meaning 'sacred knowledge', are the first-known Hindu texts, which were 'revealed' to anonymous wise sages, perhaps around 1500 BCE. There are four: Atharvaveda, Samaveda, Yajurveda and Rigveda, this last the oldest of them. The first part of the Vedas prescribes rituals and hymns. The second contains the towering wisdom collectively called the Upanishads. Because the Upanishads appear at the end of the Vedas, they are also spoken of as Vedanta.

The Upanishads—there are ten primary ones—explore the non-dual unity of the universe. They examine the relationship between the self and the world, deconstructing individual identity and connecting it to a larger whole.

Each Upanishad's entry point is a dialogue between two people, say, father and son or wife and husband, making the teachings real, accessible, almost tender. Each one is complete, reiterating the same truth through varied imagery and reasoning. Together, they create a powerful symphony of universalism, a persuasive vision of the underlying unity of all beings.

These are masterpieces that thread together intellect, emotion, aesthetics and storytelling. They are nuanced in language and tone, bringing cerebral ideas and faith onto the same page. There are no prescriptions, nor commandments. They encourage you to reach conclusions through the rigour of logic and negation. They are infused with a spirit of wonder and inquiry.

The Upanishads contain answers to the questions that haunt us in times of suffering, or even in moments of immense joy that we know, at some cellular level, will not last. Who am I really? Why am I here? And what is my relationship with the world? How can I find lasting peace and happiness?

The Vedas and the Upanishads are insights that came as revelations to seekers while they were meditating in forests, caves and mountains. Over the centuries, they have been passed on from teacher to student in a remarkable oral tradition that continues to exist outside mainstream education. Some scholars transcribed them into written texts with commentaries, a significant contributor being Adi Shankaracharya, who was born in Kerala in the eighth century BCE.

I marvel at how this literature transcends authorship and ownership, especially in this era of self-promotion. Note to self: stay grounded.

The two grand epics, Mahabharata and Ramayana, are infused with the same philosophy as the Vedas, but they are located in a particular time and place and filled with human stories and emotional upheavals. A mother betrays her son, cousins commit fraud on one another. On one level, these are the original family soap operas; on another, they are guidebooks on ethics, choices and the law of consequence. The stories contain many coded messages and many of the character archetypes in them continue to populate our worlds. The noble Yudhisthara was also a fallible people pleaser, the righteous Bheeshma was crippled by his rigidity. Karna shows us how a dominant narrative about childhood abandonment can dictate your actions throughout life unless you are able to shake it off.

In fact, the Mahabharata has been called the fifth Veda because it features the Bhagavad Gita, that life-changing dialogue between Arjuna and his charioteer Krishna on how to navigate the complex battlefield of life. The Bhagavad Gita contains the essence of the Upanishads—you are not who you think you are, know yourself—and offers a road map for how to be the best version of yourself: do what you have to do with dispassionate objectivity; see the bigger picture instead of putting yourself at the centre of every story; know that you are a mere instrument in a vast drama where truth will always prevail. It is a manual for living, really. If explained correctly, it feels like therapy.

Originally composed in Sanskrit, these epics were retold and rewritten in many languages, incorporating local cultures and traditions. For some, Karna is the hero for rising above caste-based discrimination. In certain places, the Devi is more beloved than the male gods. In other parts, Ravana is not considered a villain but a great king.

A cameo character like Janaka, Sita's father, teaches us detachment, how to be fully engaged in every duty and role without getting entangled in any of them. He had rubbed the oil of knowledge on himself, so no situation or person could touch him. Long before the Bard of Stratford, he knew that reality is a dream, that all the world's a stage, and men and women just players. The malleability of these stories does not take away from the abiding truth that shines through their core.

Valmiki's Sanskrit Ramayana was recast as the Ramcharitmanas by the poet Tulsidas, who lived in the sixteenth century. If the original was dhrupad music, this was a lighter thumri, lilting and lovely. It was written in Awadhi, the language widely spoken at the time and a precursor to Hindi. To reach a wider audience, Tulsidas also used some Urdu, describing Rama as 'Garib Nawaz', or friend of the poor, a recurring phrase in Sufi poetry.

Epic poems like the Ramcharitmanas or the Hanuman Chalisa were written to be recited, enabling even illiterate folks to access philosophy and faith-based literature. They moved out of the realm of the educated elite into an oral performative space, introducing quirky elements like the long dialogue between a crow called Kakbhushundi and an eagle called Garuda. Was this Tulsidas's way of suggesting that you can learn wisdom from a scavenger bird, a subversion of the traditional pecking order?

Garuda: What is the greatest religious merit mentioned in the Vedas and what is the worst sin?
Kakbhushundi: To take an oath of non-violence is the highest religious merit known to the Vedas. And there is no worse sin than speaking ill of others.

The Ramleela continues to be enacted just before Diwali across north and central India. A worker in the home of one of my friends has made it clear that he needs a month off during the Dussehra festival every year to play the role of

Hanuman in his village's annual Ramleela. The stories and characters in the Ramayana have grown to become universal and beloved. In a village called Kunra in Chhattisgarh, for instance, a Muslim shopkeeper plays Ravana, which he considers a great honour.

Finally, there are the Puranas, literally meaning 'old'. They contain stories that bring alive the nuances of Vedantic philosophy through dramatic situations and characters. Kings, queens, goddesses and animals become cryptic symbols and moving metaphors. The stories gently nudge us to challenge our version of reality, enabling a more fluid one that delves into parts of ourselves that we cannot ordinarily reach—like those micro-notes that coil around the more perceptible notes in Indian classical music. They contain elements of fantasy and altered realities, like a Salvador Dali painting or a poem by T.S. Eliot. A goddess turns into a river and a wise man into a crow. There is humour and poetry, dialogue and riddles. Some stories are sculpted with audacious leaps of imagination that challenge our notions of time and space, like the story of the avatar who maps the entire cosmos in three steps. A parable about ants is a reality check even for the king of the gods. There is often an allegorical quality to these stories within stories within stories, like hyperlinks on the internet that take you down rabbit holes.

Much has been written about the Bhagavad Gita, but it is the Upanishads and their vision of oneness that drew me in. We live in a claustrophobically stratified world, reduced to labels and divided by so many hierarchies. But the essence of Hindu philosophy is a celebration of the interconnected nature of all beings. It leads us into enlightened self-interest based on an understanding that the self is also the whole—like a wave that has individual form and a finite life span, but is also the ocean. The ocean contains all waves, past present and future.

The Upanishads explore the equation between the wave and the ocean—the self, or the You, and the That. Three words encapsulate this vision: You Are That, in Sanskrit, *Tat Tvam Asi*. Or *Aham Brahmasmi*, I Am Brahmn.

It became apparent to me, after studying some of these texts with Neema, that to get into this space, I would have to first slowly dismantle my idea of self, the I that appears first on the birth certificate and now, of course, on the Aadhaar card, and gets embellished with all the various roles we acquire and the labels we cling to—daughter, mother, author, Indian, clever person, arrogant person? Hmm. I have been each of these, as the context required. But it was time to take it all away. Strip down to the 'I' that lies beneath them all.

On the other side of the equation is 'That'. The closest definition for it, for it is hard to put into words, would be a permanent unchanging consciousness, or 'Brahmn'.

Balancing the equation between 'You' and 'That' is the core of the Upanishads. You and your consciousness are the same. Namita is the envelope of name and form given at a moment in time. In another round, she could have been a rose. Or the bumble bee that hovers around it. Or the mud beneath.

I am that constant observer behind a changing flow of thoughts.

I am the one that remains fully awake even when in a deep, dreamless sleep, when both my identity and the world have ceased to exist.

I am the one that abides even after death.

Most of life's pursuits revolve around becoming this, becoming that. We tend to miss the point: it is also about knowing. Once this knowledge becomes our framework, all the 'becomings' sparkle with meaning, and we begin to treat life with a sense of wonder and gratitude.

I believe that the Upanishads are India's most precious offering of ideas to the world, certainly greater than the Kohinoor that Indians periodically bleat about. The ideas cradled in these texts are radically different from what the modern world feeds us. But, despite being thousands of years old, they are also astonishingly contemporary and can be applied to ecology, psychology, biology, quantum physics in our present time. Personally, they are enhancing all dimensions of my life and giving me a clearer understanding of my own practices, big and small, from why I compost the kitchen garbage to why I am not frightened of death.

Dear reader, if you are wondering what all this means, know that not knowing is the greatest gift, for that is where the journey begins.

As the same fire assumes different shapes
When it consumes objects differing in shape,
So does the One Self take the shape
Of every creature in whom he is present.

*– Katha Upanishad**

---

* From *The Upanishads* by Eknath Easwaran, published by Jaico Books, 2010.

TO BORIVLI VIA PRINCETON

After spending four years studying in America, I returned to Mumbai, and instead of taking over the world as was expected of me, I took the slow train to a place called Borivli. I wanted to become a Hindustani classical singer. My parents were aghast, but too cool to question my resolve. So, they did the smart thing: they supported me and suggested that I give myself a year to figure out if this was really what I wanted.

The back story is that when I was ten, my mother sent me to learn music from a reclusive musician called Dhondutai Kulkarni. She lived in a single room with her elderly mother. Her entire life was contained within the pistachio-coloured walls of her home—tanpuras, tablas and a doll's house-like altar inhabited by many little gods and goddesses, always decorated with a sprinkling of flowers that were fresh and fragrant like her. Dhondutai's world was so different from mine that I turned it into my private fairyland.

Instead of greeting her with a singsong 'Good morning, Miss', I would touch her feet and she would bless me. I was initially irritated by this performative dive because it suggested servility, hierarchy, an outdated tradition. I had been raised with a sense of autonomy. But Dhondutai always had a wise response to my chronic irreverence.

'When you bow down, it forces the other person to bless you, even if they are your enemy,' she said with a laugh. 'What's wrong with collecting blessings? Before the battle began in the Mahabharata, Arjuna went across to the enemy camp and touched the feet of his grand-uncle Bheeshma. It was a clever move.'

I gradually discovered that this ritual of surrender was the preamble to learning. Inside the music room, I was taught the secret of breath control, the technique of throwing the voice and so much else—lessons not just in music but in life. Reaching the note was as important as the note itself. The path was the destination.

The teaching was intact and complete. There was nothing to add, nothing to take out. One of the meanings of 'Upanishad' is 'sitting near' (the teacher). I could have been sitting at the feet of a teacher a hundred years ago. There were no texts, no tests; my teacher used to make tea for me, chatting away about this and that, comparing the blend of two kinds of tea leaves to composite ragas. She coaxed notes out of me like a loving grandmother. She was not merely my music teacher, she unspooled for me an entire world view.

There was an interesting cast of characters in Dhondutai's world. Her tabla accompanist, Padhye master, was a favourite because he was always chatting about music, imbuing it with all kinds of ideas. In between lessons, he would talk about the temporal structure of Indian music, how it echoes the cyclical movements of everything in nature—inhalation and exhalation, the seasons, the rhythm of sunrise and sunset, life and death.

Every tabla beat structure is circular. It starts and ends at the same point and the melody plays out in between the cycles, he would say. 'It is the ongoing creation and dissolution of the universe, the breath of Vishnu.'

I have often wondered why all those years of sitting cross-legged under a slow fan, bellowing out a wordless 'aaaaaaa' (while my friends seemed to be having far more fun doing anything but this) impacted me so profoundly. Why did I stay inside the 'music room' long after I stopped singing?

Looking back, I realise that the notes and ragas were incidental. The music, and how it was taught, had coded within it a metaphysics that remained with me even after the song was over. Without knowing it, I was being taught the essence of Hindu philosophy. Maybe I was looking for a kind of earthing after returning from the US and this had come close.

Much like the scriptures, this complex musical system has sustained over centuries, without ever being written down. While it may have changed over the years, confidently absorbing influences along the way—many of the performative embellishments came with Mughal patronage, for instance—the integrity of its original intention remains: this music is an expression of devotion, a prayer to something beyond the self. It is essentially breath, the singular version of an infinitely expanding and contracting universe.

Before every lesson, Dhondutai spent an excruciatingly long time tuning the tanpura. She treated the instrument gently, as if it were a child. I would watch in wonder—and some boredom—as she twisted the knobs on top of the stem and pulled the threads on the gourd, until the four strings were in perfect harmony. The tanpura, when strummed, plays the mesmerising drone that is the backdrop for all Indian classical music. Brahmn.

'This hum is that continuum that exists even when there is no song, it is from which all emerges and unto which all retreats,' Dhondutai said to me at least a hundred times. It is the constant. It is the unchanging, absolute reality that is mentioned in the scriptures. 'Even while the voice or instrument can touch different notes and melodies, those are like your sense perceptions, they are real, but they are limited. The unwavering drone of the tanpura is the abiding sound. Know that. Hold on to that.'

'There is one concert etched in my memory,' Dhondutai told me one day. 'I was with my teacher Kesarbai, and we had brought all the instruments on to the stage. They were all a bit out of tune—tanpura, tabla and sarangi. Kesarbai then laboriously started tuning the tanpuras. First one, then the other. I could see the audience getting fidgety. But they really didn't have a choice. Then, for the next five minutes, all she did was play the tanpura, now perfectly in tune. And guess what! All the instruments fell into tune on their own, aligning with that hum.'

I listened to her whimsical stories, chuckling silently, unable to understand their full meaning. Her ragas were goddesses who had to be pleased; the presence of an enemy musician could make your voice suddenly lose its sheen. But it was an enjoyable suspension of disbelief.

There was implicit reverence for the intangible. And, over the years, in that little music room, amidst those imperceptible micro-notes and deities and the vibrations that linger long after the music is over, I embraced a gossamer play of light and shadow that revealed a non-reality, leaving nothing as it seemed.

My first few lessons revolved around singing the foundation note, sa. It had to merge with the drone of the tanpura.

'Sa drowns out all the other voices in your head,' said Dhondutai. 'It centres the body and mind and draws the breath into a steady rhythm.'

She said, 'You have to please the spirit that lives in this note.'

I began to realise that the word 'note' merely describes a musical frequency, a pitch, a melodic interval. In Western classical music, the notes are discrete and identifiable, which is why the music can be notated, written down.

Swara, in Indian classical music, is not the same thing. The notes unsung hovered close to those being sung, adding that barely perceptible tinge, that penumbra of sound. As important as the main note are the inscrutable micro-notes that coil around it. How you reach a note is as important as the note itself, for you may have to caress that almost-note that hovers next to it, evoking a completely different sound than if you were to meet the note directly.

'Swara is a living deity. You must follow it, and respect it, and then it might turn around and look at you and enter your voice, if you're lucky,' Dhondutai told me, with a chuckle.

The Western hunger for the perceivable and provable satisfies the rational mind. Eastern thought trusts the unknown and the unseen more than what is available to the senses.

'*Raag, saag aur paag kabhi dubara same nahin hai*,' Padhye would repeat in a monotone. Each time you sing a raga, cook spinach or tie a turban, the result will be slightly different. And that makes room for flow, for imperfection, for impermanence.

No one musician can take ownership of the music she sings, only partial aspects of it, like a composition or a specific style. The same raga, with the exact same notes, might be sung differently, not just by different musicians but even by the same musician the next time around.

'Our music doesn't belong to anyone,' said Dhondutai. 'A particular artiste may have written a composition or have mastery over a raga.' But the aakaar itself is so abstract, it is beyond lyrics, beyond authorship. Not one person can say, 'I wrote the aakaar'.

To me, most motivations in the West are about celebrating the constructed ego self. The essence of Hindu philosophy leans into how to spend your life obliterating it.

When I was older, I asked Dhondutai to explain the metaphysics of sound. She said, 'It is entirely contained in the sacred monosyllable, Om. It is how the world started, and it is the sound that sustains even when there is no sound. It is like the hum of the tanpura—all the instruments and the voice must align with it.'

I understood, but it still sounded complicated. Om is ubiquitous, but I had never really paid attention to the curly-wurly symbol. It was how some people auspiciously started the first page of their notebooks; my cook had a crooked Om tattooed on her forearm; and all Punjabis seem to unearth an Ommi chacha in their extended families.

A few months later, I got what I was looking for, but not from Dhondutai. She led me to it. We were in an obscure town somewhere in Maharashtra, where she had an afternoon performance in an old wada. In a cavernous hall, blue and dull gold geometric floor tiles seemed to reflect the ceiling, where the same shapes were sculpted into the plaster. A balcony on the mezzanine floor wrapped around the hall. Oil paintings of maharajas and musicians hung along the walls and there was a gigantic liver-spotted Venetian mirror at the very end.

An elderly man in a white shirt and white lungi, with a white turban wrapped around his head, sat on a red velvet chair. He looked like a Sufi saint who had stepped out of one of the paintings just for that day. Dhondutai touched his feet before heading to the stage. She called him Babaji.

Later that evening, we walked across a field of corn to Babaji's house—three rooms around a square courtyard. I noticed a tanpura covered with a white muslin sheet inside one of the rooms. We had entered a black-and-white period film!

She turned to me and laughed. 'Babaji is the right person to tell you about Om. It comes from our rishi-munis, from our Upanishads ...'

Babaji muttered 'Allahoo' under his breath. Then he proceeded to give me a sermon on the primordial sound.

Om is the beginning and the end.

The whole universe comes from Om, exists in Om and dissolves in Om.

All creation is set in motion by the vibration of Om.

Om is that continuum that exists even when all speech stops, all thoughts cease and all organs stop.

Om is consciousness, the unchanging, all-pervasive, immortal, undifferentiated force that cannot be described in words. And you are that ...

Dhondutai smiled when she saw my face. She seemed to have a clear understanding of what he was saying, as if they were both operating at a different frequency in that twilight hour.

'Om is Aum. All sounds are generated from this vowel and consonant combination and all names are some combination of these sounds. Our worlds cannot exist without names or words. Names describe everything in the world. Ideas and thoughts are communicated through words. Experiences are expressed through words. If someone utters the words "banana tree", you immediately know all about the banana tree—its shape, its leaves, fruits, the season in which they ripen. Just as an object is known through its names, so also Brahmn, or consciousness, is known through Om.'

Babaji got up from his seat, walked over to a small desk and pulled out a scrap of paper from the drawer. I jumped up to see what he was writing but could not understand his calligraphic handwriting. AUM, he said, and began explaining the waking, dreaming and deep sleep states that explain our true nature. This is what I think I heard him say that evening.

A is for *aakara* or physical form, the manifest world made up of many objects that we see in our waking state. U is *ukara* or the subtle body, that which manifests in our dreams. The impressions of the waking state are like a movie taking place on the flat screen of the mind, although the forms seem real and multi-dimensional. The dream experience taps into a deeper layer of the mind, and it feels as though the events are completely real while they are taking place. M is *makara* or the causal state, constantly in a state of potential, which exists when you are in deep sleep, when there are no dream objects, when the senses are dormant. In this state, all experiences have become one, there is only consciousness full of bliss. It is a state in which there is no sense of individuality.

Babaji was now reading out from a notebook, his eyes moving right to left, for that is the way his script travelled. Behind him was a miniature painting of a young Mughal prince kneeling in front of a Hindu priest with a river flowing behind them. A purple dusk enveloped us as we sat there, lulled by his voice, and the chalky smoke of dhoop pervaded the room.

'Just as a bird, tired of roaming, flies to its nest with its stomach full, so the person tired of the actions of the world in the waking and dreaming states, enters this state of bliss. All the experiences of the waking and the dream states melt or dissolve or become unified with the experience of deep sleep. They are not annihilated but remain in a seed state, as potential, just as a tree exists in a seed.' Babaji's voice had the soft rumble of a man who had lived through many seasons.

'Who is the "I" that remains aware even when you are in the deep, dreamless sleep, and is aware when you wake up from it? That is the all-aware consciousness that we call Brahmn. Deep sleep is the time when the individual Atman merges with the infinite Brahmn. You are that. An enquiry into the self leads into an enquiry into the universe—that is complete knowledge."

'This is from the Mandukya Upanishad,' Dhondutai said softly.

By now twilight had surrendered to an inky sky. From the corner of my eye, I saw a young man cross the courtyard towards us and go into the adjoining room. He peeled the muslin off the tanpura and started strumming it, as if offering a background hum to Babaji's voice. He started singing the lower scale of raga Yaman, moving like a slow tide into higher notes.

'Om is called Omkara by the Sikhs, Allahoo by the Muslims and Elohem by the Jews,' said Babaji. 'Om contains all the music of the world. The humming of the bees, the sweet singing of the birds, the seven notes of the scale, the sound of the drums, the lion's roar, the lover's song, the cobra's hissing, and the orator's speech, all emanate from Om. It is the music of silence. It continues even when there is no sound.'

Babaji got up, touched my head and muttered, 'Wahdat al Wajud'. He walked into the music room and briefly became a silhouette framed against the window. A few minutes later, two voices were singing in perfect harmony as one.

When I woke up, I was lying on a low couch next to Dhondutai. She had covered me with a light grey shawl. The music had stopped. Who was he? Was he a saint or a singer? Or was it all a dream?

In the end I did not make music my profession. A year after I began my excursions to Dhondutai, I accepted defeat. I did not have the stamina for such rigour, such unconditional commitment. I joined *The Times of India* and started my career as a journalist in the historic precinct of Bori Bunder, amidst gargoyles and neo-Gothic spires and the comforting cacophony of Mumbai's streets. Since then, both writing and music have been my creative companions, interchangeably spouse and lover.

The music room had started out as a physical space in Dhondutai's little flat, but gradually became a room inside me. A room we must all carve out for ourselves with a sign written in invisible ink: No Entry!

Many years later, when I was back in Borivli, drinking tea and chatting with Dhondutai, I asked her to reveal the secret two-note taan of the Jaipur gharana. Would she please finally teach it to me, now that I was so much older?

She looked at me and chuckled. 'You've been singing it since you were a child!'

She made me promise that I would keep the secret and then revealed it to me. I could not believe it. It was one of the first things I had learnt as that little girl sitting at the feet of her master. She had installed it firmly into my vocal cords so that it became the bedrock for all arpeggiated movements that I would ever sing. I truly had been singing it all my life without knowing it.

Suddenly, the flickering lightbulb came on and illuminated everything. The truth is always latent within. A teacher helps you shed the veil of ignorance. When the fruit is ripe, it falls on its own.

In the blue of the sky, in the green of the forest,
Whose is the hand that has painted the glow?
When the winds were asleep in the womb of the ether,
Who was it roused them and bade them to blow?

– Sri Aurobindo

Yeh kaun chitrakaar hai, yeh kaun chitrakaar ...

– Song from V. Shantaram's 1967 film
Boond Jo Ban Gayi Moti

HOTEL ANANDA RAMANA
NO.75/A, CHENGAM ROAD (OPP. RAMANAS
TIRUVANNAMALAI - 606 603.
GSTIN:33AANFH6114H1Z7 PH: 70944665
FSSAI NO: 22421480000121
Cash BILL
NO. 214
Time:01:57

GRIHASTHA

UNIONS, REUNIONS

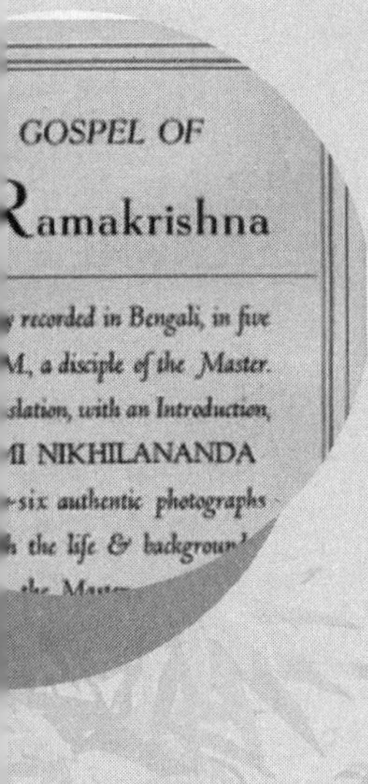

Love is a word that has been so overstretched that it is not a surprise it keeps breaking. I wonder what makes two souls mingle or collide—as lovers, friends, or even strangers.

Star-gazers say that three things are written in one's destiny—birth, death and marriage. I had to put the jigsaw puzzle pieces together to figure out my own 'it's complicated' status.

I gradually discovered that it was not that complicated.

THE FIVE ELEMENTS

There were two words I had never heard until I got married and entered P's family home: Advaita and Vedanta. Suddenly, Hinduism was not just about listening to stories about Rama or praying to Krishna. I found myself being steered into the magical stepwell of non-duality where you can drown without dying.

Before women had access to therapy, they often turned to religion and gurus to help them navigate difficult families. My ma-in-law Hardevi battled the trauma of early widowhood and overbearing patriarchy by turning to god. But rather than sitting passively in front of a statue, she found her way to the non-ritualistic altar of Vedanta philosophy. She studied the Bhagavad Gita and translated it into Sindhi, patiently writing in the Arabic script, for she had attended school in pre-Partition Karachi.

Hardevi was a hybrid of ascetic fakir and fifties cinema heroine. Her silver hair had a tinge of aubergine, achieved by her peculiar habit of massaging carbon paper into it. Her skin was translucent from papaya-skin rubbings. From her I received both beauty hacks and wisdom nuggets.

Conversations always felt like they had been stir-fried with a seasoning of magic realism.

'I move around in the biggest vehicle there is,' she would say with a shrug, turning disadvantage into privilege without ever having read Victor Frankl, and before you could ask her if she meant a Mercedes, she would say: 'The local train!'

She spent her life teaching this wisdom to many homemakers, doctors, professors, children. And when she finally lapsed into a blurry state of dementia, all she remembered clearly was this knowledge—like a bridge player might remember only his game or a violinist her fugues—not her children's names, not even her own name. The metaphysics of Vedanta had touched an indelible space, or perhaps had given her the most joy and peace. She remembered these teachings, along with random vignettes from her childhood, as if, in the end, nothing else really mattered.

This was when I began to realise that there were many shades of tangerine in this ancient faith. It was once about bowing down to nature; at some point it also became about temples and rituals. It is as much about lighting a little flame in solitude as it is about dancing and singing with robust devotion amidst other pilgrims. It has been distorted for personal gain, manipulated for self-aggrandisement. It has also given solace in times of great need. Hinduism is wide open for reinterpretation, governed only by laws of consequence, not morality. And underlying it is the extraordinary transformational Vedanta philosophy.

I asked myself, why had I never encountered these ideas before, this vision of oneness, this yoga of objectivity? Why was it kept in some secret chamber only accessed by renunciates in remote mountain caves or depressed women who found in it a salve?

P's family lived in an old bungalow called Gyan Ghar in Khar, a leafy suburb of Mumbai. Scattered through the house were remnants of glory days, including a stuffed tiger that had been shot by an enthusiastic uncle when such things were permitted, and many old rusty microphones bearing the iconic Chicago Radio crescent moon which once amplified India's freedom movement.

A vast hall on the ground floor of the bungalow had been turned into the informal family temple. Portraits of turbaned saints and wise men, some of whom had visited and blessed this home, including Chinmayananda and Anandamayi Ma, hung on the powdery walls. Marble busts of ancestors looked out of pupil-less eyes. The floor was covered with old dhurries, faded from exposure to the uncompromising Indian sun. In a small anteroom lay the Guru Granth Sahib, the holy book of the Sikhs, its pages as delicate as parchment. It had been brought all the way from a dusty town called Larkana in Sindh, carried with the same stealth and care of old-time travellers stitching gold coins into hidden pockets.

Every Sunday evening, since the 1940s, this hall had resounded with music and prayer. People from around the neighbourhood congregated with family—or maybe to get away from family. They clapped, sang along, some beautifully, others blithely out of tune. Half notes and off notes were permitted in that twilight hour before the gods. This was an Indian take on Sunday church gospel.

'I dreamt of a daughter-in-law who sings because music is a shortcut to the divine,' Hardevi said. She loved music. Her day began with Vividh Bharati, the national radio station which once roused the country with a morning raga or a devotional hymn, to set the tone for the day.

I did occasionally sing in this temple—haunting Kabir poetry that had been composed and sung by Veena Sahasrabuddhe, Shubha Mudgal and the great Kumar Gandharva, whose voice soared like the swan he sang of, and pierced that empty but full space of the shunya ghar. His music continues to defy categorisation or genre. It is beyond even music.

Kabir sang the earthy version of the Upanishads, using simple images from daily life:

> *O potter, you think you are kneading clay,*
> *but you will return to that very mud.*
> *O gardener, you can water the plants every day*
> *but you have no control over when the fruit will*
> *ripen and fall to the earth ...*

Since the Nobel Prize has now recognised that songwriting qualifies for the literature prize, Kabir would be an eligible posthumous candidate. His poetry is irreverent and mildly angry, yet lilting and filled with love. It is a cry for sanity. It questions blind faith. It challenges self-righteous critics. It keeps bringing people back to the idea that we are all going to end up in the same place, pulverised by the universal grinding mill, or plucked by the immortal gardener.

My favourite Kabir bhajan is *Ghat Ghat Mein Panchhi Bolta* ... You are the garden, you are the gardener, and you are also the one who makes the flowers wither and die, says Kabira. You are the all.

The very same force creates, sustains and destroys our fleeting lives. Every second something new is created, every second something old is destroyed, and in between, there is seeming stability—seeming because we cannot actually see our old cells die, nor experience the earth spinning on its axis. The trilogy of Brahma, Vishnu and Shiva—of creation, sustenance and destruction—is a homogenous force that fuels the endless cycle of life.

Even in my late twenties, I had begun to get a sense that the more things change, the more they stay the same. It is both humbling and liberating to know that. As Kabir's Sufi alter-ego Bulleh Shah sang: *Tu bas jhoom jhoom jhoom* ... Dance. With abandon.

Kabir was like an invisible wise parrot perched on my shoulder, a ghostly bestie with whom I instinctively connected. He seemed to pop up at different points in my life when I was feeling low. Sometimes he helped mitigate matters of the heart, sometimes he was the balm of reason, such as after the communal riots that cleaved Mumbai in 1992 and 1993. He reassured us with his words—we all came from one place, walked on one road and then confused ourselves by allowing the road to split into many roads of religion, caste, wealth ... But we will end up back on the same unifying road, in the same place. His simple logic was perfect, poetic.

Everyone draws water from the river banks
but no one draws water from where there are no banks.
No bank is the bank of Kabir
*The one who draws water from there becomes pure.**

I rediscovered Kabir's vision of unity, love and transcendence a few years later through a folk singer called Prahlad Tipaniya, and I followed him to his village, Luniyakhedi, in Madhya Pradesh's Ujjain district.

Tipaniya was a math teacher in a village school, belonged to a lower caste and drew water from a separate well. But when he sang, 'Where have you come from, where are you going, O brothers', I noticed how neighbours, priests, cows and dogs were all magnetically drawn to the music, as if they had no control over their own bodies.

One evening, Tipaniya and his sons were singing on a stage set up in the middle of the corn fields. Thousands of villagers from the surrounding areas had assembled to listen to them. The women sat on one side, the men on the other. The farmers, who otherwise guarded their wells and temples from people they deemed inferior, also arrived one by one,

---

* Linda Hess's translation of Kabir sung by Prahlad Tipaniya. https://www.youtube.com/watch?v=cApx92qpFks&list=RDcApx92qpFks&s tart_radio=1.

dissolving artificial barriers, to immerse themselves in his music. Later that night, a woman in a fuchsia pink sari got up, pulled her veil over her face and began whirling with abandon—quite likely the opposite of how she conducted herself in daily life. She could have been at a Grateful Dead concert, knock knock knocking on heaven's door.

I once asked Hardevi how something as abhorrent as caste could find place in a philosophy that upholds a vision of unity.

'My dear, even the most enlightened human beings sometimes forget the bigger picture and get caught in the intoxicating, seductive, terrifying web of maya. But you know the story of Adi Shankara and the Chandal sweeper ...'

Of course I didn't, though some vague images of a man in tangerine got resurrected from those afternoons when the television screen was black-and-white and we coloured stories with our imagination.

So, I listened to the story again. One day, Adi Shankara, the scholar who wrote the most extensive commentaries on the Upanishads, was walking towards a temple in Varanasi when a sweeper crossed his path. He instantly asked him to move away. This was the sweeper's response:

'What are you trying to push away? Do you want a body made up of the five elements to move away from another body made up of the same five elements? Or do you want consciousness to move away from consciousness?'

Shankara was stunned and stopped in his tracks. The man continued, 'Is there any difference between the reflection of the sun in the Ganga and its reflection in a well that is located in the quarters of the outcastes? Or between the space inside a gold pot and in a mud pot? What is this illusion of difference in the form?'

'The one who possesses this knowledge is my guru, regardless of whether he is a priest or a sweeper,' said Shankara, embracing the sweeper and then falling at his feet.

'It is believed that the sweeper was Shiva in disguise,' said Hardevi. 'Your lessons keep coming from unlikely places. Pay attention. This is the mystery of the universe.'

It was in Gyan Ghar that I learnt how to sing the Nirvana Shatakam, written by Adi Shankara. I had no idea at the time that from this one song sprang the entire philosophy of Vedanta. By unpacking what you are not, he leads you to understand what you are: Shivo Hum. You Are That.

Mind-intellect-thought-ego I am not, Nor ears, tongue, nostrils, or eyes; I am not the five great elements; I am Pure Consciousness, Bliss, the Self; I am the eternal Shiva.

The vital-air I am not, Nor have I anything to do with my body's physiological functions; Nor am I the speech hands or the feet ... I am the eternal Shiva.

I have neither likes or dislikes, Nor covetousness or greed, Nor I have any arrogant vanity nor any competition with anyone; I have no duty, no desire for wealth, lust or liberation ... I am the eternal Shiva.

Sin or merit can never touch me, Joy and sorrow cannot contaminate me; I know no mantra, I have no sacred pilgrimage to make, I know no scripture, nor rituals; I am neither the experiencer (subject), nor the experienced (object), nor the experiencing ... I am the eternal Shiva.

I have no fear of death, nor have I any caste or creed distinction; I have neither father nor mother for I am never born! I have no kith or kin, I know no guru, nor am I a disciple ... I am the eternal Shiva.

*Thought-free am I, formless my only form; I am the vitality behind all sense organs; Neither have I attachment to anything, nor am I free from everything; I am all-inclusive ... I am the eternal Shiva.**

This method of negating everything is the Upanishadic pathway to the revelation of the true self, the unchanging eternal consciousness. Let me attempt to show you how.

This song is made up of words. By itself, each word is a non-song. Many non-songs come together to make the song. The song will not remain the same song if every alternate word is pulled out.

To put it differently, a body is made up of cells. Each cell is a non-body. Many non-body parts come together to make a body, but if some of those parts are removed, it will no longer be the same body. A group is made up of members, but each member is a non-group until it becomes a group. A mother is not a mother until her child is born.

---

* Adapted from *Nirvana Satkam* by Swami Dayananda Saraswati, published by Arsha Vidya Research and Publication Trust.

Everything that you think you are is dependent reality which is constantly changing. The absolute reality is the consciousness that abides before, after and during this play of forms.

So, there is no objective reality in the phenomenal universe other than Brahmn or pure consciousness. Because everything can be broken down into something else. What you think you are is really not that, not that. Anything that is variable, changing and can become something else is not reality, according to the Upanishads, which says that only that which is unchanging is real.

Shankaracharya was suggesting, in more abstract terms, exactly what Kabir would come to sing—the idea that rituals and pilgrimages are redundant, all you have to know is your true nature. You are Shiva: an audacious idea for many faiths which enforce the separation of the self from god. When the Persian Sufi mystic Al Hallaj said, 'I am the Truth', he was put to death.

The vision of non-duality that Shankara and Kabir spoke of oddly does not contradict the existence of the many gods and goddesses that populate Hindu mythology. All the deities are projections of different psychological facets that are within us, not outside. Ganesha symbolises wisdom, Laxmi is the goddess of prosperity, Saraswati represents knowledge. And the overarching umbrella trinity of Brahma, Vishnu and Mahesha as creator, preserver and destroyer suggest that everything is born, sustains and resolves back into a whole, without the boundaries that otherwise separate the birth and death of the body.

In the Bhagavad Gita, Krishna reveals his all-encompassing self to Arjuna: 'I am the self that resides in all hearts. I am creation and sustenance and resolution.'

This is where abstract Hindu philosophy and the practice of Hindu religion merge. Hinduism believes that wherever there are forms, there is also the formless consciousness. Therefore, the devotee is able to unflinchingly pray to a rock and a basil plant and fire and the moon, even to a snake. Each of these elements of nature has been personified into a deity. The functional universe is also turned into god. The carpenter prays to his tools as if they are his god. Farmers sing songs about god while harvesting their crop. A musician touches her instruments with reverence. My music teacher believed that god resides in each note.

Even personal attributes are personified into god-figures. Rama is the embodiment of duty, while the mischievous Krishna celebrates our playful nature, encouraging us to tread lightly and helping us to see that devotion can take many pathways. Every god is accompanied by his or her personal animal, perhaps as a way of incorporating all creatures, great and small, into the universe of faith. Lakshmi has an owl by her side; Vishnu lies on a giant snake; the sweet Ganesha travels on a mouse. Some gods are themselves animals, like Hanuman the monkey or Nandi the bull.

When we were young, my parents used to take us on summer holidays to little towns in the foothills of the Himalayas, because anywhere else would have been too hot. We went for walks amidst aromatic conifers, and my mother always carried her sketchbook and painted gorgeous water colours of trees or snowy mountains or little temples. I specially remember the ones she did of the wayside shrines that were sprinkled across the countryside, often a mere smudge of tangerine and vermillion on a stone. There was an abstract quality to these little totems: form becoming formless becoming form becoming formless.

This translation of everything—sentient, insentient, man, woman, animal, mineral—into the divine is brilliant, for it codifies ways of being that help you navigate the universe with care, affection and respect. At least, that is the idea. It does not always play out that way because the human mind has an uncanny ability to control, distort and destroy.

By my forties, I was getting more and more drawn to this new idea. And, in a small way, I started to observe much of the world through the counter-intuitive filter of Vedanta. Every aspect of life appeared in a new light and made sense in a way I had never before imagined. I would find glowworm glimmers of this in the most unusual places, like when I went to visit my cousin, who cultivates bees in her mountain home in Himachal Pradesh, and from a poor man called Aish Mohammed, who lives behind a garbage dump in the coastal town of Alibag where I had a home.

If you were driving around the dirt roads in Alibag, the coastal idyll across the harbour from Mumbai, you might have run into a skinny man whistling to himself, pedalling along on an old bicycle. Tied to the cycle behind him, astonishingly balanced, were usually a couple of sacks filled with discarded objects—the accumulation of his day's labour. They contained anything from scrap metal to glass bottles. Aish could tell a lot about an area's demographic trends based on the trail of debris left behind, a strange but sure way to get a glimpse into consumption patterns. He could see that villagers had stopped brushing their teeth with neem twigs and were opting for the single worst offender in the plastic waste ecosystem, the toothpaste tube. Of late, he had noticed many more beer cans and foil food containers lying along the village roads like shiny roadkill. '*Aaj kal, bahut tourist jantaa aati hai*,' he said. The tourist traffic to this coastal town had shot up, and so had the quality of garbage.

The village recycler's work is a tiny microcosm of the way the universe functions—breaking up and repurposing all things. Aish discarded nothing except the label 'garbage'. He did not judge even the most disgusting piece of trash because in it he saw potential for transformation. Plastic refuse could be broken down into pellets and become T-shirts; paper was pulped to make bags.

Aish Mohammed's world was a deep study into a fundamental concept in physics as well as philosophy: matter cannot be created or destroyed, it simply changes form. He knew the secrets of a perpetually recycling universe. In nature, there is no such thing as waste. The tree that falls down and starts rotting is not dead wood but disintegrates into a source of nutrition for a future tree. Atoms from a star that was born billions of years earlier could be inside your body today, creating haemoglobin. Water is the best example of matter migrating, from cloud to rain to stream to glacier, but never disappearing. The maturing, transformation and disintegration of everything in nature is a lesson for all.

Aish turned rubbish into gold. His wife Aisha spent her days patching scraps of waste cloth into quilts. Small squares, big rectangles and torn borders came together to create a gorgeous new entity. There was a matter-of-fact approach to their craft. They seemed to know that everything in the universe serves some purpose.

Aish and Aisha Mohammed were part of a community which our twisted exploitative world has rendered invisible even though they deliver a critical service. They live in a shed behind mounds of garbage, steel on one side, glass neatly stacked on the other. While helping organise local garbage drives, I interacted with them and learnt about India's fascinating garbage trail. Inspired, I developed an interest in waste management and, along with some friends, started exploring ways in which we could lower our garbage footprint. I discovered composting. My cousin had started persuading Delhi's biggest temples to convert their daily mounds of flower waste into compost instead of dumping it in the Yamuna river. Floral waste reduced and the farmers from Haryana and Uttar Pradesh got free 'holy' fertiliser, 'khaad prasad'. Sometimes, the solutions can be simple.

I, too, started composting my vegetable waste using an earthen pot. My balcony became an experimental lab for reincarnation! I saw smelly, rotting kitchen waste turn magically into nutritious aromatic fertiliser that would be used to nourish the plants which, in turn, would give me fruits and vegetables that would benefit my body. Very simply, we are the banana and the banana peel, the mud, and also the tree. Each sustains the other through a meticulously organised, interdependent system that uses the laws of chemistry and physics to enable breath, food, life and even death.

Much later, during the Covid lockdown, I noticed a bunch of baby papaya plants growing out of my flowering pots. It was bougainvillea plus papaya, fern plus papaya, hibiscus plus papaya ... I was astonished, for papaya happens to be my favourite fruit. In those end-of-the-world times, nothing was surprising. Were we now going to be decimated by a papaya pandemic? Was this nature's revenge Part Two? I kept trying to make sense of this botanical infiltration.

The answer struck me as I was dumping wet trash into the composting pot one morning. Evidently, some papaya seeds had remained dormant in the compost that would go into all my potted plants. The magic of nature was unfolding right there. You never know where a seed of life is going to land, for it is so minute, so subtle in its presence and its potential. It carries within its almost invisible form entire realms of possibility. The seed is potentially the tree.

The Chandogya Upanishad describes a conversation between Uddalaka and his son Svetaketu, whom he instructs to fetch him the fruit of a banyan tree. He then asks him to break it open.

'What do you see there?'

'Seeds, Father.'

'Now break open those seeds. What do you see?'

'There is nothing, Father.'

'Son, I can see that you do not perceive the subtle essence that contains the yet-unmanifest banyan tree. Believe it, my son. Everything that exists has its self in that subtle essence. It is truth. It is the self. And you, Svetaketu, are that.'

A seed has to give up its 'seedness' to become a tree, just as you have to give up your sense of smallness to know that you are the complete whole. 'Is the acorn better than the oak which is its fullness and completion?' asks Ralph Waldo Emerson. Quantum physics reduces everything to atoms, particles and waves. The Vedantic view is that everything breaks down into something else, that everything is perennially in a state of potential.

❧

The dialogues between father and son in the Chandogya Upanishad contain many more metaphors drawn from nature. Uddalaka tells Svetaketu that bees gather nectar from various flowers and store it in the hive, but the honey is one. Similarly, all beings merge into a single consciousness; their individual personality is relevant, but not the complete truth.

I marvelled at how tiny elements and processes from nature had found their way into these scriptures. Spiders and banyan trees were not merely viewed through the clinical lens of botany, but as little stories that opened a window into an extraordinary higher intelligence.

When my cousin showed us nine bee boxes laid out in the midst of an apple orchard in the pine-fringed slopes of Mashobhra, I could only think about these ideas. The bumble bees were pollinating the orchard—a happy side effect being that we got fruits—and sustaining life with their nonchalant buzzy brilliance. They were acting out a simple allegory for diversity as unity: no drop of honey could possibly say, I am from this flower or that. Within one drop was the essence of so many flowers, just as within one atomic space of infinite consciousness exists all experiences.

The fresh, delicious, caramel-coloured honey that we brought back home from the mountains was a gift from the gods containing all the wisdom of the universe.

I was never good at science, but here is my simple analysis of what is going on in the world that houses all known life. Every single manifest form, from a plant to honey to a human being, is some combination of the five elements—earth, wind, fire, water and space. These five basic ingredients are arranged in different permutations to create an astoundingly diverse universe. So, a rock may be more earth than any other element, while a bee is more water. Humans are mostly water.

In India, we have long believed that elements have healing properties. We draw our energy from them. We need sunshine to produce the minerals that are essential for our body. There is an inexplicable feeling of contentment that comes from being around a body of water or inside a silent forest. Many communities worship fire. In Tamil Nadu, there is even a temple dedicated to the most elusive of the five elements: space. A bare room, with a garland of fresh flowers decorating the door.

The Upanishads say that the five sense organs have been created from these five elements—taste comes from water, touch from air, sight from fire, smell from earth and sound from space—to enable one to transact with the manifest world.

But this empirical reality is dependent on the absolute reality: Brahmn. The passing bliss of eating a bar of dark chocolate is different from the abiding bliss of disconnection from the physical body and mind, which is what happens in deep sleep.

According to the Upanishads, the truth lies embedded in the three states of living, i.e., waking, dreaming and deep sleep. In our waking life, we are connected with our minds and bodies; when we sleep and dream, we are connected only with our minds. That state is as real as the waking state, for our dream hunger is satisfied by our dream food. The dream life—where we travel to Paris or miss trains or sip tea with long-dead loved ones—is as real or unreal as our waking life. However, we get fooled into believing that our waking life is more 'real' because of the continuity of seeing the same person in the mirror every morning. That very consistency is what feeds the greatest deception of all.

It is during deep sleep, when the physical, the mental and all causality disappear, that we get a sense of the true self. We wake up feeling rested and blissed out. Who was the being that experienced that deep, restful comfort, when neither the mind nor the body was active? Eternal consciousness. That is who you are, and the body merely a lovely costume!

In deep sleep, we are 'like one unknowingly walking back and forth over a buried treasure', says the Chandogya Upanishad, suggesting that our attachment to the world of forms prevents us from realising our true selves. Bliss is our intrinsic nature. Recognise that. Embrace that. Live that.

The Brhadaranyaka Upanishad says:*

As a great fish swims between the banks of a river as it likes, so does the infinite Self move between the states of dreaming and waking.

As an eagle, weary after soaring in the sky, folds its wings and flies down to rest in its nest, so does the infinite Self enter the state of dreamless sleep, free from all desires.

The Self is free from desire, free from evil, free from fear …

The compound manifest form will inevitably decay and disintegrate. That pot you believe to be your amazing, powerful self is going to break down into mud, along with other pots, when breath becomes air. What remains is eternal bliss—the bliss that you come closest to experiencing in deep sleep.

I doubt there is any other spiritual philosophy which celebrates deep sleep so profoundly. We have all experienced that state of bliss at least a few times in life, and then woken up to the marvellous nonsense of daily life!

The rich
will make temples for Siva
What shall I,
a poor man,
do?

---

* From *The Upanishads* by Eknath Easwaran, published by Jaico Books, 2010.

My legs are pillars,
the body the shrine,
the head a cupola
of gold.

Listen, O lord of the meeting rivers,
Things standing shall fall,
But the moving ever shall stay.

*– Basavanna**

---

* From *Speaking of Siva*, translated from the Kannada by A.K. Ramanujan and published by Penguin Classics, 1973 (r. 1985).

THE TAO OF P

Although P and I lived apart for years, I could not fully understand why we always remained close. It was partly because of our son, whom we jokingly called the C-link between our homes in north and south Mumbai, but I suspect there may have been something more. We would sometimes go on secret dates. We were also periodically nasty to each other. In fact, in some ways, we continued to behave like many married people; the difference was that we could retreat to our respective homes and slowly learn how to self-partner.

My friends and well-wishers tried to nudge me to neatly wrap it up, find closure, and 'move on'. But I found out, while hurtling through life, that so much is not really in one's hands. The 'shoulda coulda woulda' is often a pointless excursion of the mind that can cause needless havoc if not reined in. After a while, I stopped resisting what was unfolding, things over which I evidently had little control.

I knew our connection had something to do with P's spiritual seeking, triggered by his own suffering and sense of unbelonging. I could see that inside the restless musician was a deep soul and an authenticity allied with an X-ray vision into bullshit. There were no masks here, and his intense transparency could get a bit overwhelming at times because we don't really want to see the truth in ourselves or in others. It is so much simpler to Photoshop our way through life.

Falling in with the expectations of those around us, I slipped into the persona of the 'good girl' and P easily fell into the 'bad boy' one. But the truth lies in a field way beyond categories. At some subterranean level I knew that the calm ocean and the restless stream are the same—they are water. The sun reflects equally on both. In this space, there are no heroes or villains. 'Maybe there ain't no sin and there ain't no virtue, they's just what people does.' How uncanny that, thousands of days ago, I had written my college application essay based on this line by John Steinbeck in *The Grapes of Wrath*. I was exploring moral relativity even as a clueless seventeen-year-old. Steinbeck's best friend, Edward Ricketts, a marine biologist and philosopher, had influenced him on 'is thinking'—an objective, non-judgemental acceptance of life on its own terms.

Besides, in the minutest way, I had started understanding that everything happens for a reason. I had to find out what secret purpose this P-tug was serving.

Just as deep tectonic shifts inside the earth do not reveal themselves till much later, on the surface, life continued as before. As C grew older, I found myself living an interesting mixture of loneliness and liberation. When friends told me about how their husbands snored or their wives bullied them, I felt relieved that I was the queen of my king-size bed, but when they posted happy family pictures on Facebook, I would feel sad.

I buried myself in productivity, while P buried himself in music and other heady intoxicants. I wrote articles and books and travelled to litfests, while P, when he wasn't bending notes on his harmonica, went for Vipassana meditation or to Ramana Maharshi's ashram in southern India. I never really understood those excursions. We were chasing different dreams.

Yet, I was always intrigued and would listen intently to what he had to say about his travels, trying to understand his interest in something I viewed as vaguely ancient, definitely unconventional. It challenged my sense of self and humbled me. It forced me to introspect and question my own certainties.

Over the years, P would send me cryptic messages like: 'Don't come in the way of your Self' and 'Wake up from the dream'. I could not make sense of them, and truthfully, they sounded a bit unhinged, but they were also more interesting than 'Let's go out for brunch'. I would go through the unusual selection of books on his shelves, including *The Tao of Physics* and a hauntingly illustrated book called *Be Here Now*. He would gift me books and scribble messages like, 'Sometimes, you may have to just take the leap and build your wings on the way down ...'.

We had music in common and listened to Kumar Gandharva and Muddy Waters with equal joy. 'Saturday midnight blues morphs into Sunday morning gospel,' said P. 'There is no need to separate them—the dark and light of life. They remind you to embrace every part of yourself because that landscape is the truth. Those guys in the Mississippi Delta were sublimating their suffering into music. That's how you get gospel gems like '*Walk with me, Lord ...*'.

A part of me thought he was loopy, a part of me was angry with him, a part of me loved him. But I instinctively paid attention to some of what he had to say. I wanted to know more about this idea of distancing yourself from the self, knowing that your personality—which you spend most of your life cultivating and showcasing—is the most beguilingly deceptive part of who you are ... I liked the idea that there is a 'you' beyond your thoughts, your feelings, your actions, so you create some distance between yourself and yourself.

The Mundaka Upanishad describes two birds sitting on the branch of a tree. One is eating the bitter-sweet fruit; the other is observing the bird that eats. You are both those birds—the one participating in all aspects of life as well as the one who observes that one. You know the bird's true nature lies beyond the volatile graph of joy and suffering.

All this turned out to be a teaser for what would come my way some years later when I plunged into a river in Rishikesh. The history–geography of my life was still taking shape, but the map was already in place.

In the Brhadaranyaka Upanishad, the nobleman Yajnavalkya decides to leave his home and wealth and go in search of truth. He tells his two wives that he is leaving all that he possesses to them so they may be comfortable for the rest of their lives, and gently asks for permission to take their leave.

His wife Katyayani accepts this. But his wife Maitreyi stops him and asks, 'What is it that you are seeking that is even greater than what you are leaving behind? Sir, if indeed this whole earth full of wealth be mine, shall I be immortal through that?'

'No,' replied Yajnavalkya. 'Your life will be just like that of people who have plenty of things, but there is no hope of immortality through wealth.'

'Tell me, sir, of that alone. I want that, not this.'

He then tenderly tells his wife that he was waiting for her to ask him this question, because you don't give this knowledge to one until a person is open to it. Even Krishna, who had known Arjuna all his life, shared the Bhagavad Gita only when his friend turned to him in his moment of anguish. And so, Yajnavalkya starts his explanation, first unpacking the name Brhadaranyaka:

Brh, in Sanskrit, means big or vast. Here, it is used not as an adjective but as a noun. Aranyaka is the forest, a perfect and biodiverse ecosystem, but also one that can be terrifying for the person travelling through it, unless she has knowledge about the self.

This Upanishad suggests that what we think we are doing for another is actually being done for the self. Even when we perform an act of charity, it's not just about helping someone, but about the joy or satisfaction it gives us.

Now, having established that it is ultimately about satisfying the self, why not invest time and effort in getting to know that 'self' better? That is how Yajnavalkya begins.

The power no longer rests with the outside object. How do you dip into the magic cauldron and make that feeling permanent, instead of endlessly seeking it outside, where it will always be short-lived and likely lead to suffering once gone?

Will finding true love make you happy perennially? Wild success? That extra zero in your bank account? All of it will, but up to a point. The love object will eventually pass away or lose its attraction; success is relative and performative; and everyone knows that 'money can't buy me love'.

If the real pleasure is coming from the self, then figure out how to induce that same feeling and make it endure regardless of the circumstances. Listening to it, the idea felt like a new, contrarian take on being selfish. But it was an enlightened self-interest.

Yajnavalkya uses different imagery to show how the 'Brh' or bigness of god pervades everything but is itself free from them all. 'Just as the drum or the veena produce different sounds, the sounds cannot exist without these instruments, but the instruments are free of the sounds,' says the Brhadaranyaka Upanishad. Similarly, the human body operates through different processes—digestive, respiratory, circulatory, and so on—but these functions would not exist without a higher intelligence behind them, which is independent of them. Again, different trees take in the same energy from the sun and the earth, but one produces mangoes and the other, unfailingly, apples. One could make an endless list of the specific 'intelligence' of different beings that draw from one source which is independent of all of them.

Human beings are grotesquely delusional, believing as they do that human intelligence is superior and can exist without the support of the universe. We forget the intelligence of fish that move between oceans in synchronised patterns without leaving a carbon footprint; or the bees that pollinate, without which we would be bereft of food. Trees give us oxygen, without which our so-called superior intelligence would not exist for even a moment. Yet, we denude entire forests and dump filth into the sea. The whole harmonious, dynamic universe of interconnected existence includes way more than one can even imagine; human intelligence is a sliver within it.

That is the difference between partial intelligence and the complete higher intelligence of the universe which contains everything, known and unknown, seen and unseen, past and present. It is pervasive, but it remains independent. That is what some call god. Or consciousness. The 'Brh' as a noun. That is what you are too. There is no duality. All is one.

The very idea of authorship—'I did this'—is rickety. There is, always, only partial authorship, and the creation wouldn't even exist if it weren't for the immortal hand or eye, as William Blake put it. Who created our creativity? Who gave biologists a scientific disposition and also created the incredible diversity of creatures and plants for them to study? Gravity existed before Newton discovered it.

I find myself increasingly baffled by human hubris. How can we believe we are outside nature and try to control it rather than align with it? I read a line recently by the American poet Nathaniel Mackey: 'Sometimes you have got to look up at the sky and enjoy the humility of just taking in this obviously superior and more complex creativity. What we do could never match that. Could I ever write a poem as intricate as a pine cone?'

I wanted more of this ...

... I did not know that I was already getting it.

When C was six or seven years old, the three of us went on a trip to Kolkata. P was playing at a music club called Some Place Else and I had a book event. We were staying at a relative's bungalow in a tree-shaded lane in Ballygunge, shielded from the Ambassadors and trams that clanked and lumbered through the old colonial city. It felt like the balmy summer holidays of my childhood, where afternoons were spent dozing on a vast bed under a slow fan, watching a lizard not move.

From Kolkata, we were going on to Sikkim. But before we took the flight to Bagdogra, P insisted on taking us to Belur Math, the spiritual centre established by the saint Ramakrishna Paramahamsa. I don't remember much about this excursion, perhaps because I had no idea who he was, beyond a mention in my school history textbook. But I have some vague recollections of the trip—steps leading down to the Hooghly river, the Kali temple, a silent hall and a portrait of a beautiful woman called Sarada Devi, in a white sari, her hair cascading like a waterfall over one shoulder.

I also remember the taxi ride from Ballygunge to this place. The driver was from Bodh Gaya and spoke in a Bihari dialect, delighting us with every lyrical turn of phrase. He chattered about his family, his goats, and how he had a hotline to Shiva. He told us how a policeman had been harassing him for speeding, but then got caught taking a bribe! 'Poor fellow lost his job,' he said, sounding genuinely sorry even for one who had troubled him.

Then he addressed C. 'Babu, do you know the story of the ants?'

My little boy looked at him quizzically, because it clearly was not a part of his usual story roster.

'A boy, about your age or maybe a little older, once showed up at the door of Indra, the king of the gods, holding a staff and a bowl. Indra was in the midst of building a palace that was vast and filled with lush gardens and terraces. Every time the palace looked like it was complete, he would say he was still not satisfied and kept asking for more, more, more ...'

Before he could finish his story, we had reached our destination, so it was left unfinished. I thought I would look it up and tell it to C while we were travelling in Sikkim. But, driving along the Teesta river in a land where the trees outnumbered people, silence seemed more articulate.

We were headed to a town called Pelling, which was known for the monastery where Buddhist monks still did their thing. We were welcomed everywhere by fluttering prayer flags that sent blessings into the wind. We entered the monastery in time to see a row of young monks in burgundy robes chanting like a chorus of crickets. They sat against a backdrop of fading frescoes depicting many Bodhisattvas amidst the curly clouds that drift through all Tibetan-inspired art. The young waiter in our hotel said that he had also spent a few years in the monastery studying various subjects, from chemistry to Buddhist values.

Every morning, we hoped that Kanchenjunga would reveal herself, but the clouds were stubborn. We sighed, climbed lesser mountains and sampled a variety of momos and steaming thukpa soups. On the last day, after we had given up on a sighting, the skies cleared and we woke up to the full majestic splendour of Kanchenjunga emerging from a halo of celestial cotton wool. Within ten minutes, she was clouded over again. She was right there, but I had not yet learnt to see through the veil.

I have only a blurry recollection of this trip, of the saint of Belur Math, the painted monastery, and the ants marching in precision on a dusty road in eastern India. There were so many other things that were turning our little family topsy-turvy in those days that the universe must have slipped a to-be-continued bookmark into the story of the ants.

Who was this Ramakrishna?

Ramakrishna Paramahamsa was born Gadadhar Chattopadhyaya in 1836 in a village called Kamarpukur in rural Bengal. When he was a little boy strolling in the fields, he looked up at the sky and saw a flight of snow-white cranes against a dark thundercloud. He was so struck by the sheer beauty of god's creation that he fainted.

As he grew older, he remained a childlike mystic. He once jumped around pretending to be a monkey and even urinated from atop a tree, all to dissolve the idea of differences and worldly etiquette. His constant underlying motivation was to reveal the unity of everything. He behaved like a madman and sometimes a child. He believed that children embody the innocence of non-duality—not differentiating between pure and impure—and any person who knows god develops the temperament of a child.

Ramakrishna's worldview was expansive and inclusive. There was a time when he would repeat the name of Allah and mutter Islamic prayers several times in the day. His mysticism invoked Christianity and he had visions of Jesus Christ. He pointed out the similarities between the Buddha's teachings and the Upanishads and showed great respect for the Sikh gurus. In his room, there was a small statue of the Jain Tirthankara Mahavira and a picture of Christ, before which he would light incense every day, morning and evening.

'A lake has several ghats. At one, the Hindus take water in pitchers and call it "jal"; at another, the Mussalmans take water in leather bags and call it "pani". At a third, the Christians call it water. Can we imagine that it is not jal, but only pani or water? How ridiculous! The substance is One, under different names, and everyone is seeking the same substance; only climate, temperament and name create differences. Let each man follow his own path. If he sincerely and ardently wishes to know God, peace be unto him! He will surely realise Him!'

Ramakrishna was so averse to limiting his identity to his body that he would sometimes wear just a loincloth and cover himself with ash. At other times, he would dress in women's attire and dance because he believed that the feminine mind had greater devotional intuition. He was gender-fluid. He was awake, not 'woke' as we know it today. He embraced members of the lower castes and rejected the scriptural arrogance of priests. Sometimes he roamed around cremation grounds in the middle of the night. For Ramakrishna, the world was filled only with god in varied forms. He would unflinchingly repeat: Accept whatever is happening. Not a leaf moves without god's will.

I 'met' Ramakrishna through his talks and parables, which had been compiled into a book that fell into my lap thanks to P. Published in 1942, *The Gospel of Sri Ramakrishna* was edited by the writer and professor Joseph Campbell, who became involved with the Ramakrishna Centre in Manhattan's Upper East Side.* The writer Aldous Huxley wrote in his foreword that this book 'where discussions of the oddest aspects of Hindu mythology give place to the most profound and subtle utterances about the nature of Ultimate Reality, is in itself a liberal education in humility, tolerance and suspense of judgment'. The text was edited by Margaret Wilson, the daughter of Woodrow Wilson, a former American president. She eventually moved to Pondicherry to be with Sri Aurobindo, the revolutionary poet, philosopher and scholar of the classics who had also been moved by the writings of Ramakrishna. In 1936, she wrote a letter to him: 'The strongest desire of my heart is to reach the only goal worth striving for, the consciousness of union with the Highest.'

The Gospel chronicles the talks given by Ramakrishna as he moved around Bengal. No interpretation, no

---

* *The Gospel of Sri Ramakrishna* was originally recorded in Bengali by M, a disciple of the Master, and was later translated by Swami Nikhilananda, who also wrote an introduction. It was published in 1942, with a foreword by Aldous Huxley.

explanations. It's straight from the source. And it is rare to come upon writing that is so erudite, yet so accessible.

'Once, a salt doll went to measure the depth of the ocean. No sooner did it enter the water than it dissolved. Now who could tell how deep the sea was? The one who was meant to tell had itself dissolved.' Arrogant, ignorant human beings think they can measure the ocean when all they can do is dissolve into its infinity.

Here is one of my favourite stories from the book:

> Near a monastery, a monk saw a landlord mercilessly beating a poor man. When he tried to intervene, the landlord took his rage out on him and started beating him, until he fell unconscious. When the monks found out, they carried their brother back, nursed him to health, and gave him a little warm milk, which helped him get conscious again. At this point, one of the monks said: 'Let's see if he can recognise us.'

He shouted: 'Revered sir, who is giving you milk?'

'Brother,' replied the holy man, in a low voice, barely audible. 'He who beat me is now giving me milk.'

When Ramakrishna was asked, if god exists in all beings, then why are some people cruel and why do so many people behave in such irrational ways, he said that god exists in all beings as the all-pervading spirit, but in some places, there is a manifestation of the power of knowledge, in other places, of the power of ignorance. 'Don't you see that among human beings there are cheats and gamblers, to say nothing of men who are like tigers. I think of them as the "cheat god" and the "tiger god". They have to be saluted from a distance!'

This idea was echoed by Aurobindo years later. While he was imprisoned in Kolkata for participating in the freedom struggle against the British, he wrote: 'I looked at the jail that secluded me from man and it was no longer by its high walls that I was imprisoned; no, it was Vasudeva who surrounded me. I walked under the branches of the tree in front of my cell but it was not the tree, I knew it was Vasudeva, it was Sri Krishna whom I saw standing there and holding over me his shade ... I looked at the prisoners in the jail, the thieves, the murderers, the swindlers and, as I looked at them, I saw Vasudeva ... I looked, and it was not the Magistrate whom I saw, it was Vasudeva, it was Narayana, who was sitting there on the bench.'

In the course of time, Sri Aurobindo went from being a freedom fighter to one who was engaged in a battle for another kind of freedom, one that could resist the colonisation of the mind.

The many little pieces of the great Indian jigsaw puzzle of mysticism started falling into place. Among those who were enormously inspired by Ramakrishna was a young man called Narendranath, a graduate of Presidency College. He later became known as Swami Vivekananda, the monk who gave Indian spirituality an exalted place at the Parliament of the World's Religions in Chicago in 1893. Addressing a massive congregation, he spoke with reverence for all religions and quoted from the Bhagavad Gita: 'Whosoever comes to me, through whatsoever form, I reach him; all men are struggling through paths which in the end lead to me.'

The relationship between Ramakrishna and Vivekananda was truly a merging of urban Western rationalism and earthy Eastern mysticism. Vivekananda used a more reasoned approach to explain Vedic thought to a Western audience. He explained how the body which we believe to be the self is nothing but a combination of perishable material substances; the true self is imperishable. He urged every individual to focus on that imperishable universal self in order to be truly liberated, to be happy. The idea, he said, was to replace 'this miserable little prison individuality' with 'infinite universal individuality'. He constantly referenced Christian ideas and saints and stated that Indian thought respected different approaches to spirituality. He also said in one of his lectures: 'The best thermometer to the progress of a nation is its treatment of women.'

There is something so incredible about the wisdom that emanated from him and something so regrettable about it not having been taught to us, along with math and music. To me, it felt like the beginning and the end of all knowledge. Yet, I knew so little. It was starting to feel like we had been learning irrelevant, complex algebra without mastering the basics: like 1+1 will always equal 2.

Today, there are more than two hundred Vedanta Societies affiliated with the Ramakrishna Mission across the world, which teach and serve human beings, regardless of which god occupies their altar. I know that no one who enters the Ramakrishna Mission in Santacruz, a suburb of Mumbai, looking for treatment at its clinic, or solace in its meditation hall, is turned away. Somewhere along the way, I also learnt that Hardevi had donated her entire collection of books to the library in this serene campus. A child, in some later decade, may learn something from one of those books, just as one might find shelter under a banyan tree planted by an unknown benefactor a hundred years ago.

For me, great saints such as Ramakrishna Paramahamsa or scholars like Aurobindo had always been reduced to postage stamp-like images, identified vaguely as important Indian personalities. They were quaint but dated, like typewriters and vinyl. Or like statues with pigeon droppings on them—Vivekananda, tall and turbaned, hands folded across his chest; Shankaracharya always seated cross-legged with his head covered; Chaitanya Mahaprabhu dancing ecstatically with his arms raised. Yet, they mattered and popped up in our lives like that leaf that emerges out of a crevice in a concrete wall. C was named Chaitanya.

In my forties, I was finally looking beyond the caricature and had started reading and re-reading their works. It soon became apparent that they all led to the same place, deviating only in approach, emphasis or tone. Some were scholarly and articulate, while some others used the language of mystical poetry. Yet others were cocooned in the bliss of devotion. Some among the devout became saintly. Tukaram. Gnaneshwar. Basava. Kabir. Narayana Guru. The Buddha and Guru Nanak founded religions that derived from the philosophies of ancient India but rejected the stultified Brahminic dogma and orthodoxy that had crept in. The Mughal Prince Dara Shikoh had translated the Upanishads into Persian before he was beheaded by his brother, Aurangzeb. All of them were arriving at the same place via different routes, on bullock carts, airplanes, boats, and sometimes only travelling in their minds. No visa required. In fact, followers of this philosophy have not been confined to India and definitely not to Hinduism. Saint Francis of Assisi, a Christian mystic, believed that everything and everyone was part of a whole. In more contemporary times, an American priest called Richard Rohr speaks eloquently about how folks can connect with this whole or be forever unhappy.

I intuitively knew that following the wisdom of these teachers didn't require me to relinquish reason. Rather, it led to a more valuable, more expansive use of my reasoning mind.

These saints are the lighthouse beacons of an India that has long existed, quietly and powerfully resilient to many forces that have pounded on its doors. Sometimes, it seems that their wisdom is in danger of being swept away by the dry desert sand of cell phones, with a side order of French fries and divisiveness.

Or, maybe not.

I was beginning to discover that there were still many who were comfortably tuned into this frequency—from the illiterate to the erudite—and they were authentic in their spiritual expression, like the whirling dervish oblivious to his audience. These seekers are often invisibilised or mocked by a society that applauds shallow celebrities more than the little old lady who feeds the birds every morning or the villagers who dance and sing their way to the house of god. *Vithala Vithala.*

While new doors of perception were opening, the brain has a way of falling back on default options. I had been raised to keep religion at arm's length. I called myself secular. I was not sure where I was heading with all this. So, I slowly started seeking reinforcement and validation for my tangerine love affair from sources beyond Hinduism, beyond India, even. It was while browsing through P's bookshelves that I stumbled upon three brilliant thinkers who had been moved by the wisdom of the rishis—a psychologist, a physicist and a philosopher. Each has left a legacy that has been transformative for many, and will be so for those still to come.

The Psychologist

In the early sixties, when Americans were having a national meltdown, struggling with a leadership that believed in violent victories over mindful living, it triggered various kinds of pushback. One of them was a lava-like movement towards Eastern mysticism.

Richard Alpert was then a bright young professor of psychology who taught at Harvard and had research contracts with Stanford and Yale. He had achieved, even by competitive Jewish standards, enviable success at a very young age. He drove a Mercedes Benz, had his own Cessna airplane and vacationed in the Caribbean.

'But,' he says in his book *Be Here Now*, 'what all this boils down to is that I was really a very good game player ... my lecture notes were the ideas of other men, subtly presented, and my research was all within the Zeitgeist—all that which one was supposed to research about.'

Alpert's association with his colleague Timothy Leary drew him to the use of psychedelics, and he started experimenting with mood-altering substances like mushrooms and LSD. But he realised that every time he got close to a new, higher consciousness, he would come down back to his old state and lose the experience. His predicament was that he wanted to remain there, to make it a permanent cognitive lens, a new approach to old living. At some point in this excursion, he lost his job at Harvard and gained what he called a psychological rebirth.

Then he came to India.

Through a series of unplanned events, he arrived at the foothills of the Himalayas, and ended his journey at the feet of a wise man who was clothed in a blanket: Neem Karoli Baba. They had a few abbreviated conversations, and Alpert describes how he felt like his rational mind had exploded. Later, he remembered crying and crying, feeling neither happy nor sad. He felt he had come home, to a place where he surrendered his ego with absolute joy. 'For the first time I understood what a guru was—he was not just a teacher, he was a spiritual vehicle, an entrance to god.'

He stayed for seven months. When he was leaving, the guru said to him, 'Is there something you want?'

'The only thing I want is not to lose faith.'

Alpert knew by then that he no longer had to apply his Western cynicism, nor rely on his rational mind or his senses, to understand the total interconnected universe. This was the beginning of his journey, one that would transform him into Ram Dass. He went on to share his learnings, help others, and also understand the power of silence. He drew from the great Hindu sages as much as from Buddhism,

Christianity and from pop lyrics. His talks soon became popular all over the digital world, peppered with a wry wit that managed to make spiritual discourse almost hilarious.

When someone asked him if one can become a seeker without the guidance of a guru, he said: 'Relax. You are being guided. In fact, the next measure you need in the treasure hunt is exactly where you are when you need it. The message may be in the form of a teacher or a lover or an enemy or a pet or a rock or a chemical or a book or a feeling of great despair or a physical illness or the eyes of a person you pass on the street.'

Some years later, inspired by Ram Dass, a young American called Steve Jobs would find his way to this very ashram in the hills of Nainital though, by then, Neem Karoli Baba had passed away. The young techie was besieged by a bout of dysentery but, while recovering, he found a book left behind by a fellow-traveller that influenced him profoundly for the rest of his life. The book was *An Autobiography of a Yogi* by Paramhansa Yogananda. Jobs's biographer Walter Isaacson mentions that it was the last book he had downloaded on his iPad before he died. Isaacson writes that, while Jobs was relaxing in his garden in Palo Alto, he reflected on the lasting impact of his trip to India: 'Coming back to America was, for me, much more of a cultural shock than going to India. The people in the Indian countryside don't use their intellect like we do, they use their intuition instead, and their intuition is far more developed than in the rest of the world. Intuition is a very powerful thing, more powerful than intellect, in my opinion. That's had a big impact on my work.'

It was as if pebbles had been left behind by one traveller, then another, forming a pathway through the forest for anyone to discover.

The Physicist

Physics was my worst subject in school. I gravitated towards the Humanities, although I was always secretly fascinated by nature's poetic precision and also how music draws on mathematical patterns. I was, therefore, overjoyed to discover Fritjof Capra, an Austrian-American physicist and author of *The Tao of Physics*, who dissolved the silos between the scientific and the spiritual. He viewed the universe not in linear terms, as populated by isolated individuals who see the world as something outside themselves, but as a throbbing interconnected network of relationships, what he called 'a grand symphony of life'. He suggests that the rational mind's ability to decipher and organise is limited. It is not in touch with involuntary instincts and thus causes constant frustration to one who wishes to control outcomes. In fact, the rational part of research and discovery often relies equally on the intuition and the sudden insight that comes when scientists are relaxing—in the bathtub, under a tree, or on the beach.

Capra's epiphany came while he was sitting by the sea, watching the waves and feeling the rhythm of his breath. 'I suddenly became aware of my whole environment as being engaged in a gigantic cosmic dance. Being a physicist, I knew that the sand, rocks, water, and air around me were made of vibrating molecules and atoms and that these consisted of particles which interacted with one another by creating and destroying other particles ... at that moment I knew that this was the dance of Shiva.'

The fragmented view—separating the self from the world, and separating mind, body and spirit—is what has led to hierarchies and divisions in society, serially propelling economic, political and ecological crises. 'It has alienated us from nature and from our fellow human beings.'

Capra writes that the two major concepts of modern physics—quantum theory and relativity—both nudge us to see the world the way a Hindu, a Buddhist or a Taoist sees it.

'Every molecule in our body was once a part of previous bodies—living or non-living—and will be a part of future bodies,' he writes. 'In this sense, our body will not die but will live on, again and again, because life lives on. Moreover, we share not only life's molecules, but also its basic principles of organisation with the rest of the living world. Indeed, we belong to the universe, and this experience of belonging can make our lives profoundly meaningful.'

He explains how the natural world's interconnectedness suggests that life has evolved for billions of years using the same basic patterns and substance. Physics, chemistry, biology, the spirit, are inseparable in this complex network of relationships and self-regulating patterns.

Capra describes himself as a scientist, ecologist and activist with a holistic view of existence. 'The awareness of being connected with all of nature is particularly strong in ecology. Connectedness, relationship and interdependence are fundamental concepts of ecology; and connectedness, relationship and belonging are also the essence of spiritual experience. I believe therefore that ecology—and in particular the philosophical school of deep ecology—is an ideal bridge between science and spirituality.' His ideas have been echoed in the 'deep ecology' movement that views human beings as deeply connected with, and a part of nature, rather than entities trying to either control the environment or protect it.

For me, this approach was a no-brainer. The anthropocentric way of living—where man places himself at the centre of the universe rather than as one of many participants—has clearly had disastrous consequences, from the frightening pace of ecological collapse to the ever-increasing intolerance on display across the world. The 'ecological self' seamlessly lives in harmony with nature, abiding by the sense of interconnectedness and aware that every being, sentient or insentient, is equally valuable. How can such a person then pollute a mountain or deflect the path of a river? Is it not the equivalent of stuffing thermocol down one's own gullet?

The Philosopher

In the nineteenth century, a German philosopher called Arthur Schopenhauer read the Upanishads in Latin, which in turn were translations from the Persian. He said that nothing he had previously read was quite as elevating. He became a believer in the idea of the illusory quality of the material world and suggested that all humanity is made from a common metaphysics. He suggested that everything is meant for everyone, which meant that one was actually sharing with oneself rather than with an 'other'.

He also spoke of transcendent fatalism: as we grow older, and 'the thread of life has been spun out to a considerable length', what becomes clear is that the course of one's life, however confused and random it might appear to be, is as carefully mapped out as an epic. This 'hand of fate', as he calls it, may be moved by an external circumstance or an inner impulse, but it is perfectly organised ... Just as a turtle that has just hatched reflexively moves towards the water without being able to see it.

There are two fundamentally different things that are going on simultaneously in every individual's life: on one level, all events and situations are based on an objective cause-and-effect process of nature; on another level, there is a subjective experience which is exclusive to the individual experiencing it. The difference between 'real' life and dreaming is just this: that, in a dream, there is the ego-self interacting with others and events, but it is also the ego-self that wills and feels the emotions and actions of the other characters as well; in real life, there are many ego-selves interacting with one another. Each one is the hero of his own drama, but also figures in the drama of others. Based on what Schopenhauer calls each one's 'metaphysical guidance', the exact same event can elicit completely different feelings and responses from different people.

He talks of how it is in the creative arts that one can experience the transcendental self, the 'aah' moment. While the ego-self strives constantly to make sense of the world through logic and reason, the aesthetic experience, such as playing or listening to music, entails a 'will-less' perception which goes beyond the intellect. It is no longer about the where, why, how, but rather, simply, the what. Objectively understanding the what *is*, rather than its relation to the striving self.

One of the many thinkers influenced by Schopenhauer was an American professor, Joseph Campbell, who became obsessed with mythology and the not-so-hidden meanings that are coded in them. In his later years, Campbell used to quote Schopenhauer's belief that one often senses the presence of an author out there who is writing the novel of one's life. Although events may appear as chance, there is a well-ordered plot in place. Using this framework, he came up with the idea that you must follow your bliss, the rapture that is the only experience that one can hold on to—knowing that the life you should be living is exactly the one that you are living! As the Stoics say, *amor fati*.

The pebbles had been scattered far and wide. In the 1980s, a young film-maker in Los Angeles took inspiration from Joseph Campbell's writings. His name was George Lucas, and he created a movie series that brimmed with all kinds of ideas about life and space, good and evil: *Star Wars*.

I began to see how this philosophy is timeless and had been flickering into our lives on and off in so many ways. I felt less alone, almost as if I had joined an invisible community of astonishing thinkers and seekers.

To see a World in a Grain of Sand
And a Heaven in a Wild Flower
Hold Infinity in the palm of your hand

And Eternity in an hour
Man was made for Joy & Woe
And when this we rightly know
Thro the World we safely go

*– William Blake**

---

* From William Blake's poem 'Auguries of Innocence' (poetry foundation.org).

MURUGAN AND THE MOUNTAIN

When C was about eleven, we went to Pondicherry for a short holiday, again as a family, because that was one thing we managed to do reasonably well—vacation together. Two days after we arrived, there was a massive cyclone and everything shut down. We spent the next day slightly dazed, wandering amidst the destructive aftermath of fallen trees and shards of glass. Our trip to the town of Auroville had to be cancelled. The flight back to Mumbai was after three days. That was when P suggested we drive out to Tiruvannamalai or Tiru, his adopted native place.

Tiru wraps around the base of Arunachala, a stand-alone mountain that is geologically older than the Himalayas. It is the place where Ramana Maharshi had meditated for years, P told us. Once again, I had no idea who this person was. He sounded saintly, other-worldly. All I knew about him was a rather obscure piece of historical trivia. That at the height of India's independence struggle, when Mahatma Gandhi was driving past Ramana Maharshi's ashram, his followers ensured that he did not go in. On the strength of that random factoid, and the lure of delicious vegetarian food served on banana leaves, I agreed that we should head there.

Then, we got diverted by Murugan.

In India, ideas of right and wrong are oddly fluid, so you could be following the rules and yet be overthrown by a rule-breaker with the full support of the public—which is exactly what happened to us. While driving to Tiru, we managed to convey to the driver, who spoke no English, that we were hungry and wanted to make a quick food stop. But as he proceeded to make the left turn to Murugan Idli House, a speeding motorcycle came hurtling towards us from the other direction, resulting in a resounding crash.

Suddenly, we were inside a C-grade Tamil film, more horror than entertainer. Within minutes, like ants descending on a blob of sugar, we were surrounded by many lungi-clad men who seemed to emerge out of nowhere. Instead of breaking into a Prabhu Deva dance sequence, they shouted incomprehensibly at the driver, who sputtered that it was not his fault. The irresponsible motorbike rider suddenly became the hero, emboldened by his supporters, and was whisked off to a hospital. A couple of hefty cops drove up and sneered when I waved my *Times of India* ID card at them. No one spoke either Hindi or English. We might as well have been in Sicily.

Meanwhile, the traumatised driver decided that he could no longer take this and suddenly started shouting, mostly to himself. The only word I could make sense of in his spewing deluge was 'Murugan … Murugan'. He took our bags out of the car, left them on the porch of Murugan Idli House and, before we could protest (in a language he would not even understand), he sped off, leaving us stranded on a dusty Tamil Nadu highway.

The car company was not reachable; there were no taxis in sight; only trucks and tempos whizzed past us. Not one person in the little eatery spoke a word of English. It was getting dark. Taking one step at a time, we decided to first drown our sorrows in some soothing idli-sambar.

'I guess we'll be sleeping here tonight,' said P, pacing up and down the porch and turning increasingly irate. Our little boy was visibly exhausted, on the verge of tears, and asked if we could go back to Mumbai. My response to this hopeless situation was to dissociate. I went blank, leaning against a wall with my eyes shut, alternating between zoning out and praying. I opened them when the soft hum of a tanpura and a whiff of sandalwood floated towards me.

A man in a lime-green shirt and a crisp white veshti with a matching lime-green border was circling a bouquet of incense sticks in front of Shiva and Murugan, who were framed above the cash register. The sound of the tanpura emanated from an app on his iPhone. He sang 'Om Namoh Bhagavate Sri Ramana' three times with his hands folded and eyes shut, before opening them and turning to us.

'You guys in trouble?' He spoke in English, with a slight American twang. We learnt shortly after that this man in lime green, with a beard of cropped white stubble, was called Raman, after Ramana Maharshi. He was the owner of Murugan Idli House. He used to be a chemical engineer in Houston and, when both his children went off to college, had decided to move back to be closer to his village, and to the Sage of Arunachala.

An hour later, he was driving us to the ashram in his SUV, playing Crosby, Stills, Nash & Young via a novel technology called Bluetooth. Within minutes, little C fell fast asleep with his head on my lap and a hint of a smile on his face. Maybe he was dreaming of the dancing peacocks that he was about to see in the ashram.

We are one person
We are two alone
We are three together
We are for each other…

There is an old Tamil saying: 'To see Chidambaram, to be born in Tiruvarur, to die in Banaras or even to think of Arunachala is to be assured of liberation.'

Just before the turn of the twentieth century, a skinny young boy called Venkataraman left his home in Madurai and took a train to Tiru. He spent the first few years in the thousand-pillared hall of the Arunachaleswara Shiva temple and later moved to a cave in the mountain where he stayed, meditating, barely eating. His family entreated him to return home, but he remained there, believing that silence was also conversation. He then wrote a note to his mother:*

> The Ordainer controls the fate of souls in accordance with their past deeds. Whatever is destined not to happen will not happen, try how hard you may. Whatever is destined to happen will happen, do what you may to

* From www.gururamana.org.

stop it. This is certain. The best course, therefore, is to remain silent.

Eventually, his elder brother and mother moved there to be with him and became his disciples. His mother cooked every day, serving the villagers and the monkeys and squirrels that would gather around this strange, silent man who did not differentiate between animals and humans. Venkataraman became Ramana Maharshi—Bhagavan to many—and stayed in Tiru till his death in 1950.

Once, when asked, 'Bhagavan, how should we treat others,' he replied, 'There are no others.' He believed that everything offered to others is really an offering to oneself; and if only this truth were realised, who is there that would refuse anything to others? Even snakes were his companions when he meditated inside the cave.

The most common question asked to him by students was: how can I accept that the world, which I am sensing all the time in so many ways, is not real? To this, Ramana Maharshi's answer was: how can the knowledge of objects arising in relative existence to one that knows not the truth of himself be true knowledge? If one rightly knows the truth of him named 'I', in whom both knowledge and its opposite subsist, then along with ignorance, (relative) knowledge will also cease.

When Ramana Maharshi was asked how people could do things to help the world, he said: 'Helping yourself, you help the world. You are in the world; you are the world. You are not different from the world, nor is the world different from you. Just as the spider draws out the thread of the cobweb from within itself and withdraws it again into itself, in the same way the mind projects the world out of itself and absorbs it back into itself.'

The definition of reality according to the scriptures is: that which exists unchanged and without intermission. It is not in time, nor in space. It is neither a cause, nor an effect. It has an independent reality. This, he stated repeatedly.

Ramana Maharshi said, whatever burdens are thrown on god, He bears them all. Since the supreme power of god makes all things move, why should we, without submitting ourselves to it, constantly worry ourselves with thoughts as to what should be done and how, and what should not be done and how not? We know that the train carries all loads, so after getting on it, why should we carry our small luggage on our head to our discomfort, instead of putting it down in the train and feeling at ease?*

In the 1930s, at the height of the nationalist freedom struggle, Mahatma Gandhi came to Tiru to give a political speech very close to the ashram. He had planned to visit Ramana Maharshi afterwards and even cut his speech short to do so. But as their open car slowed down near the ashram gates, the Congress leader C. Rajagopalachari, who was travelling with Gandhi, gestured to the driver not to stop. He was concerned that once Gandhi entered the ashram, he may never leave, and might forget all about

* *Living by the Words of Bhagavan* by Sri Annamali Swami, translated by Sundaram Swami, edited by David Godman and published by Sri Satguru Annamalai Swamigal Spiritual Trust..

the independence struggle. Some years later, when India's first President, Dr Rajendra Prasad, came to the ashram, he asked Ramana Maharshi for a message to take back to Gandhi. 'The power of the true self is working within him and leading him on. That is enough. What more is necessary?' the sage replied.*

In 1938, one of my favourite novelists, Somerset Maugham, visited the ashram for a few hours. His brief encounter inspired him to create a similar character in his gem of a book, *The Razor's Edge*, whose title was very likely derived from the Katha Upanishad which says: 'Sharp like a razor's edge is the path to Reality, difficult to traverse'. In Maugham's bestselling novel, a despondent man travels the world, seeking answers, and meets an Indian guru. The protagonist Larry says of the guru: 'He never wore anything but a loincloth and yet he managed to look as trim and well-dressed as a young man in one of our Brooks Brothers' advertisements.' In the Oscar-winning black-and-white film made of the book, the production designer who, in the 1950s, probably had not the faintest idea what a simple Indian ashram looks like, conjured a Greek temple-like structure with elaborate columns against the backdrop of a fake-looking snowy mountain.

The Razor's Edge was one of the first books I gifted P, inscribed to 'the zen banker'. At some point, I hunted out the slim paperback that had survived many countries and family upheavals. The cover came apart as I pulled it out of the bookshelf; the pages were yellow and parched.

---

* From 'Talks with Sri Ramana Maharshi', davidgodman.org.

Something fell out of the book and I bent to pick it up. It was a peacock feather—blue-green, luminous and perfect.

The mountain of Arunachala is neither snowy nor majestic, but it is a living being and is considered the embodiment of Shiva. There is a story about how Vishnu and Brahma got into a fight about which of them was greater, and Shiva was brought in to resolve the dispute. He manifested as a column of fiery light, and said that whoever could find its upper or lower end would be the greater god. Vishnu took the form of a boar and burrowed deep into the earth to find the base, while Brahma became a swan and soared upwards to touch the summit. Vishnu failed to reach the end, but 'began to see within himself the supreme light which dwells in the hearts of all'. Brahma found a ketaki flower and tried to deceive the others by saying that he had plucked it from the summit.

Realising the truth of this light without beginning or end, Vishnu turned to Shiva in praise and prayer: 'You are Self-knowledge. You are Om. You are the beginning and the middle and the end of everything. You are everything and illuminate everything.' Brahma, meanwhile, confessed his mistake.

In this legend, Vishnu is supposed to represent the intellect and Brahma the ego, while Shiva is the atma, the self, which requires a surrender of both ego and intellect. Just as fire remains hidden in the firestick, and oil in sesame seeds, and butter in cream, 'so dwells the Lord of Love, The Self, in the very depths of consciousness. Realize him through truth and meditation,' says the Shvetashvatara Upanishad.*

At this point, Shiva manifested as the 'Supreme Shiva', the all-encompassing one that absorbs all, takes back all, who contains Brahma, Vishnu and Shiva—creation, sustenance and destruction—while he remains in a state of perpetual meditation, untouched. There is nothing static, nothing that doesn't change. Everything originates, grows, decays and ends, ephemeral flashes in the cosmic dance of Shiva.

Legend has it that Shiva then transformed the column of light into the Arunachala hill, declaring: 'As the moon derives its light from the sun, so other holy places shall derive their sanctity from Arunachala.'

Ramana Maharshi says: 'In the end, everyone must come to Arunachala.'

And that, simply, is how we got there, to climb the mountain, to trek to the cave where the sage meditated, and to sit cross-legged on the floor and eat the most nourishing food served on giant, gleaming leaves.

It wasn't part of *our* plan, but it was part of *the* plan. The cyclone had brought us here. Not all storms are destructive.

---

* From *The Upanishads* by Eknath Easwaran, published by Jaico Books, 2010.

IMAGINE ...

I was acutely aware that C didn't have a Masterji in his life, one who could help him pause and travel in a world beyond isosceles triangles and the battle of Plassey. His grandmother Hardevi had developed dementia, and could no longer be the ambient guiding light. His grandfather Bhagwat was more inclined to discuss science than mythology. And my bedraggled copies of Amar Chitra Katha could scarcely compete with digital gaming.

My music teacher had told me that what a child absorbs before his mind is cluttered with the ceaseless chatter of thought stays imprinted. So, before his little moustache sprouted and he entered that inscrutable teenage era of perpetual jetlag, I made valiant attempts to introduce him to bits of what I knew. I read to him from a beautifully illustrated Children's Mahabharata, whose episodic stories make it perfect for bedtime. I started reciting the Hanuman Chalisa with him, verse by verse, learning the percussive Awadhi poem myself in the process. *Kaanan kundala kunchita kesaa*, with earrings on each side of his curly hair.

As long as C was young and impressionable, this benign indoctrination worked. But a ruthless version of Hindutva had started becoming the background score in our country, a perennial, growling drumbeat that spasmodically became a deafening techno-rave. The city of Mumbai had always been casually cosmopolitan and politically abstemious, so this was new and unnerving. Many of us started feeling a sense of unease over anything Hindu. How had such a profoundly sophisticated religion unleashed so much hatred?

I started noticing a certain suspicion towards my pursuits because they were to do with Hinduism. I remember meeting a group of Ambedkar scholars one evening. When I mentioned that I was studying the Upanishads, the pleasant banter instantly ceased and I was treated like an outsider.

The world was being split into reductive binaries: those who rejected religion were liberal and those who expressed their faith, right-wing. This was not entirely surprising. The feral soldiers of Hindutva were asserting a dangerously illiberal version of a faith that in so many of its complex, even contradictory stands, is enormously liberal. Between these two extreme sides was that vast majority following the fifty and more shades of Hinduism whose voice had been practically muted. It was now a Mahabharata of egos with no Krishna to save us, no Kabir to guillotine our hubris.

The human mind constantly needs to generate the 'other' to validate its own position, perpetually boxing and labelling, as if we are cornflakes. Simplify. Classify. Crucify. And yet, just as politicians will continue doing what they do, and fighters will continue fighting, I had to follow my heart.

But the damage had been done. As C got older and more discerning, he started rejecting the very idea of Hinduism, of faith. Every time I talked to him about a new idea that had illuminated me, he would get irritated and accuse me of contradicting the humanitarian values that I had always upheld. C went to a Christian school; his best friends were Jain, Muslim, Parsi. They expressed anger over exam timetables or indifferent teachers, not towards one another.

I eventually took a cue from my mother, who had led me to the music room, and took C to a space that transcends the us and them. I took him to Padhye Masterji, Dhondutai's lifelong tabla accompanist, so he could learn the tabla. Along with rhythm and beats, I knew that C would be exposed to a bewitchingly different universe.

Once, after C was done with his lesson—I had come to pick him up—one of Padhye's older students began relating the story of the butcher of Mithila in response to a recent attack on meat-eaters.

The learned sage Kaushika had anger management issues. Once, a bird pooped on him while he was meditating. In a fit of rage, he cursed it and it dropped dead. Another time, a woman kept him waiting at her door, and he admonished her. She then told him that real wisdom comes not from parroting the scriptures but living your best life. She advised him to go meet Dharmavyadha, the butcher of Mithila, to understand the real meaning of righteous living. Kaushika was surprised—a butcher would teach him dharma? His arrogance gradually surrendered to humility when he learnt that Dharmavyadha had inherited his profession, which happened to be butchery, and he was simply doing his duty and taking care of his family. Kaushika understood that there are no absolutes. Each situation calls for a different response. That is dharma.

But outside Padhye Masterji's classroom, the high tide of hatred had grown into a tsunami and we were all drowning. I remember one lesson in particular. The master was in the middle of teaching C Teentaal when we heard a distant blast. It merged into the noise of the city. A few minutes later, one of Masterji's students came running in, sweating, panting, already mourning.

'There's been a bumsphote guruji, a bomb blast. Not one, but two … maybe more,' he said.

The maestro looked up, nodded, and then continued to engage with the sixteen-beat, easing back into its cyclical perfection, tenderly sheltering and guiding the child's little fingers on the drum. Dhaa dhin dhin dha. Consistent, like the seasons. Rhythmic, like breath. Returning to the beginning again and again, as if to keep giving life a chance. A musician was passing on love, beauty, truth, so that it would outlive him. It was the antithesis of what had just taken place outside.

But by the time he got to Ektaal, another student arrived bearing more detailed news about the terror attacks. We were just a few minutes away from one of the blast sites. Although nothing could be more secure than the music room, it was time to get out of there. The road outside had already been cordoned off. Masterji asked one of the students to escort us, and we stepped out—into darkness. People were walking around in a daze, ears glued to their mobile phones. An ambulance bleated past us. As we made our way home, I watched my son react to a city having a nervous breakdown. He seemed strangely stoic, inured. Were we now living in a world where even children had learnt to normalise violence and terror? 'A' for anger. 'B' for blood.

Imagine if, every morning during the school assembly, children listened to an abhang by Bhimsen Joshi, or A.R. Rahman singing *Khwaja Mere Khwaja*, or Nirguna poetry sung by Kumar Gandharva, or a Qawwali by Farid Ayaz ... Imagine if these songs were played at railway stations. Or in prisons, like that memorable scene in the film *Shawshank Redemption*, when a prisoner plays Mozart's aria over the public address system; one by one, the inmates stop and stand transfixed by music sung in a language they cannot even understand. In those moments, they are free.

Imagine all the people ...

The secret of all the knowledge that one acquires in the world is the knowledge of the self. For instance, music is played externally, but where is it realised? It is realised within. A good or bad word is spoken outwardly, but where is it realised? It is realised within.

At the same time, the error of man always continues. Instead of finding realisation within, he always wants to find it without. It is just like a man who wants to see the moon and yet looks for it on the ground.

*– Hazrat Inayat Khan**

* From *The Sufi Message Vol 2: The Mysticism of Music, Sound and Word* by Hazrat Inayat Khan, published by Motilal Banarsidass Publishers, 2002.

போளுவாம்பட்டி – அட்டப்பாடி யானைகள் வழித்தடம்
BOLUVAMPATTI - ATTAPADI ELEPHANT CORRIDOR
யானைகளுக்கு நடமாடும் உரிமை உண்டு
இடையூறு செய்ய வேண்டாம்
Elephants Have Right of Way
Do Not Obstruct
DRIVE SLOW

VANAPRASTHA

ENTERING THE FOREST

The Sanskrit term 'Alam Buddhi' is the wisdom of knowing the state of enough. It is a space of knowing that the extra zero, or a new cuisine, is not going to add much more value.

At some point in your life, you begin to realise that greed is a mental construct and does not independently exist. You pay attention and break it down every time it bubbles up. My interior compass was looking for a new north pole—and everything seemed to lead me in its direction.

THE ANTS IN TAMIL NADU

A sari border transcribed onto stone. We were on a bus in Tamil Nadu, approaching the magnificent Brhadeswara temple of Tanjore. From a distance, I saw a row of Nandis sculpted in black stone, seated at regular intervals along the rim of the wall that fringed the temple complex. This would be the recurring pattern that I would find across south India—the elegant bulls in repose, waiting patiently like many silent devotees frozen in time.

As I entered the temple, music magically started streaming in my head; it was Ashwini Bhide Deshpande's enchanting composition on Shiva in raga Nat Bhairav. I was being wrapped in a cocoon whose threads were drawn from art, devotion and bliss in that twilight hour in Tanjavur district. It was lovely. Sometimes you have to trust a feeling. No analysis. I messaged her to share my joy and she responded with gratitude. She got it. I had already heard it in her music.

After C went away to college in America, I received a lot of well-meaning advice from friends and family: You can now write a new book or start another literary festival; you can find a new companion; you can travel much more …

I was fifty-one years old and I didn't particularly want any of this. I had saturated those aspirations—been there, done that—and there's no end to wanting more of the same. Instead, I was thinking of shifting the kaleidoscope yet again, to see new colours and designs in the same spaces. Like a certain Beatle, I wanted to arrive without travelling, see all without looking, do all without doing. My companion would be my new self, happily coexisting with the old Namu.

In the Vedic belief system, there are broadly four stages in life: you spend the first twenty-odd years as a Brahmachari or student, a celibate devoted entirely to learning. I had spent these years in very different places: with my music teacher in Borivli, and at Cathedral School, followed by Princeton, though I can't speak for the celibacy part. Next comes Grihastha or the householder stage, where you devote yourself to having a family, earning a living and looking after your home. My son's presence kept me out of trouble, and for that I am grateful.

Grihastha is followed by Vanaprastha, and finally Sanyasa. Vana literally means forest, a metaphor for the unknown, the wild, and also a place of solitude. The forest is the space where nature precedes man, and it forces you to align with it. This is where wise men over the years have spent time in contemplation and received insight—that zigzag lightning flash depicted in picture books.

These stages are not prescriptive, but broad markers that can be chronologically shifted and circumvented if the situation demands. You can marry in your sixties, join a college for higher learning in your seventies. In fact, mid-life, I was becoming a student again.

I was joyful that C would be ensconced in a liberal arts college where he could be immersed in subjects as diverse as math and music amidst woods and streams. And, instead of turning into a lonely empty-nester, a prospect that did hover over me for a bit, I realised I wanted to slowly walk towards the forest. But I had no plans to head to the Himalayan foothills, where I wouldn't last a day without my morning coffee, gluten-free bread and the comforting chatter of my besties.

The secret of the forest stage is that it is a state of mind. It is in the here and now—in practising wisdom and retreating slowly from the sly thought machine and bludgeoning emotions that keep you embroiled. It is a transition phase. It is about engaging fully, but with an understanding of what is real and unreal. Knowing that, in the eyes of god, a moment is the same as an entire millennium. Realising that the dreamer and the one awake are not that different. Vanaprastha was going to be my decade of contemplation, my attempt to tap into a different frequency. I would attempt to filter every thought, every experience, through a new understanding. I would engage with the world with detached attachment. Like the noble king Janaka, whose moment of realisation came when a bad dream seemed so real that he actually fell off his bed and hurt himself, after which he proceeded on a journey of inquiry with the learned sage Ashtavakra.

Or, like Rama. Long before the young prince went into exile in the forest, he experienced the kind of existential crisis that many sensitive youth might have. He started questioning the point of life. He wanted to renounce everything and retreat to the wilderness to get closer to god.

He plaintively asked his father King Dasharatha and the elders of his court: 'What is that secret that enables one to remain unaffected by the grief and suffering in the world, like mercury is unaffected when thrown into fire? What is that secret? What do people call happiness and can it be had in the ever-changing objects of this world?'

At that point, Dasharatha asked the sage Vasishtha to guide his beloved boy. The wise man embarked on a long chat with the prince, which has been compiled into a scripture, the Yoga Vasishtha.

'May I ask where you are right now?' Vasishtha asks Rama. 'There is nowhere which is not within the ambit of god. Renunciation has to happen in your mind. You can live anywhere ... Rama, there are four gatekeepers at the entrance to the realm of freedom, moksha. They are self-control, a spirit of enquiry, contentment, and good company.'

The Yoga Vasishtha explains each of these and suggests that the wise seeker diligently cultivate them, or at least one of them.*

The first value required for inner freedom is self-control. This is the ability to live amongst all and stay unaffected by them; it is the capacity to get neither elated, nor miserable, just as one would be during deep sleep, when the mind retreats. The second value is to have a constant eye open to spiritual enquiry, not losing sight of it even in the midst of activity. The mind is more engaged with questions like, Who am I? How has this samsara, with its repetitive cycles of birth and death, come into being? It is the absence of enquiry that gives rise to actions that are harmful to oneself—and to others, says Vasishtha.

---

* *Yoga Vasishta*, translated by Swami Venkatesananda and published by SUNY Press, 1993.

The third value is to be in a state of contentment by renouncing all cravings and becoming satisfied with what comes to one naturally, unsought. This makes the purity of the heart bloom, the sage advises the prince. 'The contented man who possesses nothing owns the world.' Finally, the idea of satsang, or the company of like-minded wise men and women expands one's intelligence, destroys ignorance and mitigates psychological distress.

These edifying ideas were beginning to make sense to me. I was quite clear that I wanted to abdicate control, surrender to wisdom and make my way to the other side.

So, I gradually turned my room into my 'ashram'; my personal forest was a languorous gulmohar tree outside one window, while a giant mango tree wallpapered the other. Every year, just before the monsoon, the gulmohar burst into a sindhuri-crimson blur and the mango tree became pregnant with fruit, mostly enjoyed by flocks of parrots who perched and squawked like entitled fine diners. Trilling squirrels were on surround sound. I woke up to birds that started singing in the dark with the faith that dawn would always arrive. I continued to eat avocado toast for breakfast like a happy non-renunciating renunciate. And I carried on in life with the new pair of lenses that my eye doctor had not prescribed.

I now considered myself part student, part householder, but I also knew that I was gradually entering the forest. Thinking about life as divided into four stages is one way for individuals to complete every dimension, engage with the emotional, intellectual and spiritual self before surrendering to the inevitable—death or freedom, depending on how you view the final bye-bye. Those who get stuck in any one stage may find themselves a bit stunted, or bored. I had seen otherwise smart people get waylaid by some blind spot and spend their lives fighting for a few extra zeros or chasing validation through some other route. Sometimes, the ego became more important than the zero.

I now had the inner leisure to float mindfully, without worrying about whether I was going to miss some dreadful parent–teacher meeting or ensuring the fridge was stocked with sausages. Even work had slowed down because of the pandemic. Everything had slowed down, enabling many to recalibrate their internal compass.

December of that year, I was back with Neema, along with my friend Shona and many others, on our annual retreat—this time in Manjakkudi, a tiny village in the Kaveri delta. This is where her teacher Dayananda Saraswati was born, in a little house with a big courtyard. This is where he spent the first seventeen years of his life before he became the 'Swamiji' that so many revered.

We drove from the astonishingly modern Tiruchirappalli airport along salubrious swathes of rice fields lined with banana trees and coconut palms. In the midst of the green, a distant dot of bright red or electric blue blared out the sartorial choice of a farmer.

On our way, we stopped at the magnificent Tanjore temple complex and admired the endless borders of Nandis, carved with masterly precision. Art, beauty and divinity collaborate to elicit humility, the first step towards freedom.

Thousands of pilgrims roamed around, praying, taking selfies, marvelling at how such structures had been built in an age before machine tools. A group of shirtless men in black lungis informed me with many head nods that they were engineers who had taken time off work for one month to go temple-hopping and end up at the feet of Ayyappa, another son of Shiva in the bottomless pantheon of Hindu deities.

As twilight descended, the Nandi bulls were silhouetted against a cobalt blue sky. Suddenly, the entire temple complex was lit up in a golden light and the music started—a version of raga Kedar was being played in the Parvati temple. A silver crescent moon smiled at the perfection of the evening. At that moment, I saw something move behind one of the Nandis. It was a peacock. He climbed on to the bull daintily and perched himself on the hump for a few minutes, also in silhouette, an ephemeral live sculpture. Then he turned his head and flew away.

Manjakkudi is a picture-book village fossilised in time. We had entered an R.K. Narayan world, where children rode to school on bicycles, tinkling little bells and dodging goats and cows with practised ease. The houses on either side of the single main road were exactly the way they would have been a hundred years ago, with baked-tile roofs, voluptuous wooden columns, red-oxide floors and a few banana trees in the front yard. An elderly man might be sitting on the porch with his granddaughter on his lap, teaching her a mantra. Most of the younger people had moved away and got vacuumed into the tech abyss. Some had been educated at the Dayananda Saraswati College, which has produced many distinguished alumni working at some of India's leading companies.

At the end of the road was a small Lakshmi Narayan temple, its dome dotted with gods painted in the affably garish colours that characterise temples in this part of the country. On the ground in front of every house was a cheerful rice powder kolam. By evening, the patterns would be smudged by the dust of daily life, sometimes overridden by a sprinkling of petals and goat droppings. The next morning, just after sunrise, would come the swish-swish of a broom, and then the white designs would magically reappear.

'Do you know why we do this?' Neema asked, smiling.

'For decoration?' I replied.

'To welcome visitors into the house,' suggested Shona.

'Yes, that too, but it serves another purpose. These patterns in front of the house are made with rice powder so that ants and other creatures get to eat. No animal should go hungry. Besides, if the ants are full, they will not come inside to forage for food!'

I imagined a line of ants walking away from the white patterns, well fed, chatting about the state of the earth, about how dumb human beings are, and about how they must stay away from white sugar to keep their insulin in check. I started laughing, because I remembered the parable of the ants from many years ago …

When Indra, the king of the gods, had triumphed over earth, he commissioned Vishwakarma, the god of art and craft, to build a palace complex with many gardens and courtyards. Not satisfied with the splendid buildings that had been created, Indra asked for more pavilions and more ponds, and then more and more. Exhausted with his demands, Vishwakarma turned to Brahma and Vishnu for help.

The next morning, a radiant young boy holding a pilgrim's stick arrived at Indra's palace. The king invited him in to offer him the customary honey, milk and fruit given to wandering mendicants. The boy then spoke to Indra in a voice that was deep and molten.

'I have come to see the grand palace that you are building. No Indra before you has managed such a feat of construction.'

Surprised at the idea of there being Indras that existed before him, Indra gently asked the boy to explain what he meant. The response left him with a quiet foreboding.

'I knew your father, Kashyapa, the Old Tortoise, who created all creatures, and your grandfather Marichi, the beam of light, Brahma's son, and Brahma himself, brought forth from Vishnu's navel while he breathed in the great ocean of eternity ... I have known the dissolution and creation of the universe, again and again, and how every single being goes back into the fathomless infinity of that dark ocean ... who knows how many Indras existed in all those passing ages, ascending to the throne of the king of gods and then passing away into that ocean ...'

During the boy's discourse, a procession of ants appeared and paraded across the floor like soldiers marching with marvellous precision. The boy stared at them and started laughing, then went silent. Now Indra started getting nervous.

'Who are you really, in the disguise of a boy?' he asked, stammering. 'Why do you laugh?'

'I laughed because of the ants,' the boy said. 'The reason is a secret, for it contains the fruit of wisdom that destroys the tree of worldly vanity. It lies hidden in the wisdom of the ages and is rarely revealed. It is what ascetics and renunciates breathe, but it destroys those who are deluded by desire and pride.'

Expressing a newfound humility, Indra begged the boy to reveal the secret of the ages, the light that dispels the darkness of ignorance. Since he had been requested to teach, the boy opened up:

'In that parade of ants, each ant was once an Indra like you. Like you, each ascended to become king of the gods, through virtuous deeds. But now, through many rebirths, each has become an ant again. This army of ants is an army of former Indras. It is through one's deeds that one gets to high places and through one's deeds that one falls into the lowest ranks. Death is the master of all.'

The boy (who was Vishnu) disappeared, leaving the king first baffled, then subdued. His greed to build more and more evaporated. Newly wise, he summoned Vishwakarma, told him to conclude the palace construc-tion, and sent him home with many gifts.

When I heard this story, I instantly wanted to make every real-estate builder and politician listen to it before they poured molten concrete across the planet. But then, I quickly corrected myself. The self is the only space where change takes place. The world emanates from the self and collapses back into the self. I had to meditate on the ants, observe my own choices, and annihilate the greed within.

Sometimes, I wondered whether these myths and mantras were leading me into a bubble that would insulate me from an irrational and covetous world. But so be it. This knowledge was stretching my mind to understand the hidden secrets of our interconnected lives, where even the tiniest creatures are important. An ant can be easily squashed, but if it enters your ear, you are at its mercy. A single female mosquito that lives only a few weeks can disrupt your life. Can you ever know why or when that will happen?

You don't have to be more Hindu or less Hindu to understand this. You don't even have to be Hindu. You either get it or you don't. The arrow has to hit the eye while the bird is spinning.

This year, Neema was unravelling the Mundaka Upanishad.

The student Saukata asks his teacher, what is that knowledge, knowing which all else will be known?

The teacher responds: Brahmn, the changeless absolute, from which all comes, because of which all exists, and unto which all resolves. What is, is Brahmn. You can see the world with many names and forms, all of which have different functions and roles, but if you shift your perspective, all that is here is Brahmn. Consciousness.

This is what it says: just as trees come out of the minerals of the earth, but are not separate from the earth, they go back to the earth; and just like the spider that spins a web with juices from its own body, Brahmn manifests or projects the world as well as resolves it.

You are Brahmn.

When you are awake to the manifest world, you are Brahmn, when you are dreaming, you are Brahmn, and when you are in deep sleep, the world does not exist, but you still do. How else would you wake up and feel refreshed?

Creation is, therefore, a cycle between manifest and unmanifest, just as the sprout inside the seed is an unmanifest tree that will yield seeds someday. The world manifests in cyclical movements of creation and resolution. The sama where the music begins and ends.

In between classes, we were taken around the village to see the fifty-acre farm that had been developed in memory of Dayananda Saraswati by one of his devotees, a Chennai-based businesswoman. She and her team had sourced more than two hundred varieties of indigenous rice which were becoming extinct because of the widely available high-yield, genetically modified seeds. The ashram volunteers were preserving the indigenous rice varieties in a seed bank as if they were agro-emeralds. They were planted and grown pesticide-free. Every day, we would sample the rice: Bora from Assam, Ambe Mohar from Maharashtra, Chennel from Kerala.

I could only marvel at their commitment as I went on morning walks along the luminous fields. White egrets flew in and out of the green paddy and pink lotus emerged out of ponds. As I watched the golden sun rise and heard the peacocks honking as if greeting it in their birdie version of prayer, the question would keep coming back to me: what has made us turn away from glorious nature and greenscapes to snorting concrete carcinogens? What are we all chasing with such ruthless, pointless aggression? In a pulsating '*Yeh Dil Maange More*' world, isn't simplicity the new luxury? It confounded me, and continues to. But that is the great mystery of modern life.

You have brains in your head.
You have feet in your shoes.
You can steer yourself
*any direction you choose.**

* From *Oh, the Places You'll Go* by Dr Suess, published by Random House, 1990.

WHERE ELEPHANTS HAVE RIGHT OF WAY

Many years ago, an Indian economist living in Bangkok discarded her pant suit for a white sari and arrived in a forest academy in the Nilgiri Hills, in a remote area along the border of Tamil Nadu and Kerala. Her name was Neema Majmudar and she was about thirty years old.

Neema had a Master's in public policy from Columbia University and worked for the United Nations. She had grown up in Mumbai, watching Bachchan movies and taking the train to college in Churchgate. Her pious grandparents had translated Valmiki's Ramayana into Gujarati, while her father was a firm rationalist who believed that religion came in the way of nation-building. So, like many Indians, Neema had both streams within her, flowing side by side.

Her first posting was at the UN headquarters in New York. One day, she was visiting a friend at UPenn in Philadelphia. While strolling around the campus grounds, she noticed a poster bearing the picture of a bearded man dressed in orange, staring straight into the camera. Printed below was the cryptic question: 'Do you know who you really are?'

It was not the kind of question she had encountered before. Intrigued, she decided to attend the day-long seminar that was being held on campus. A Vedic scholar called Swami Dayananda Saraswati was addressing a subject that sounded audacious: everything you think you are, you actually are not. Well, then, who are you? There, in the middle of the United States, this modern–ancient man transported his audience to an elevated Wonderland like some saffron-clad Lewis Carroll. His wisdom, his humour, the gentleness with which he spoke, his equal mastery over English and Sanskrit, moved her tremendously.

Neema returned to 44th and Lexington and continued to solve geopolitical equations, but she could not forget the talk. The ideas hovered like butterflies fluttering gently in some part of her. A few years later, she learnt that this teacher had established a traditional centre of learning in Saylorsburg, a town in Pennsylvania. She found herself magnetically pulled back to listen to his lectures, not once but several times. He was nothing like the professors she had encountered, and he seemed to be more compassionate than many of her colleagues working to resolve global humanitarian issues.

Neema asked the swami if she could join his teacher training course on Vedic philosophy. He suggested that, because she was still young, she should spend some more time working, earning and fulfilling her material aspirations. She should have no regrets later. So, she went back to her UN job, which took her to Bangkok and the Fiji Islands, but she stayed in regular touch with him. A few years later, he said: 'Neema, you are now ready. Come.'

That's when Neema arrived on a bus from Coimbatore to the Arsha Vidya Gurukulam in a town called Anaikatti, leaving behind a family who could not fathom what had just happened to their brilliant daughter's promising career track. This had never been part of the plan. But they also knew their daughter. They could see that her decision was unwavering.

Neema spent three and a half years in the forest academy along with about fifty other students from all over India. They also spent a month in the Rishikesh campus. There was only one short break when Neema went to Mumbai to visit her family, who were still baffled by her new avatar.

This is where she studied the Upanishads, the Bhagavad Gita and the distilled essence of the Vedic scriptures. The lessons were taught by the master himself. She learnt Sanskrit from a scholar with a PhD from Stanford, who had left his Silicon Valley coding job to study a very different language. Neema also learnt Vedic chants, practising each endlessly till she had mastered the correct intonations, because a single syllable could change the meaning and potency of what was being uttered.

The programme was relentless. The students had classes every day, with no break even on Sundays. They had to prepare daily summaries of what they had learnt. There was no television, nor access to newspapers, so they had no idea what was happening in the outside world. In their free time, they worked in the kitchen, washed their clothes, or planted trees.

Sometimes, when a student cribbed about the workload, their teacher simply said: 'There must be a reason you are not able to do what you are meant to do. You are mature enough to figure it out. Do as much as makes you comfortable. There are no rules because rules will restrict you from moving towards the bigger picture.'

The entire course was free and classes were conducted in English, though the students came from across India, some from cities and others from remote villages. Each came with a different story. The son of a farmer had heard a talk by an itinerant Vedanta scholar and was smitten by the wisdom of the rishis. The daughter of a professor wanted to learn about the origin of all scholarship. A young physics teacher had left her job to attend the course, perhaps sensing that she needed to look elsewhere for the final formula that would help her to make sense of the universe.

As the students became immersed in their studies, old ways of thinking fell like dead leaves to the ground. Conditioned responses were gradually replaced by a new understanding. The ego was forced to face itself in a new mirror. At first, Neema, having come from an educational system that applauds competition, was mildly chuffed to note that some of the students were not as smart as her. She noticed that one Tamil student, in particular, seemed to be faltering when they were studying the complex Brahmasutra, which contains a series of dialogues and debates between practitioners of the different schools of philosophy. While Neema was quick on the uptake, this young man was not always able to comprehend what was being taught, and kept interrupting the class with questions. One day, while the students were visiting a neighbouring town, they ran into a group of lepers, who instantly bent and touched this particular man's feet. She discovered then that the not-so-intelligent man had spent a year in the service of lepers. Any lingering sense of superiority vanished in one second. That moment taught her that scholarship without empathy was as good as carrying water to a sick man inside a golden jug that has a hole.

It was around this time that a young man from Paris arrived at the forest academy. Surya Tahora was the grandson of Shia priests who had migrated in the nineteenth century from Gujarat to Madagascar. He had just left his job as head of international sales at a pharmaceutical company to be with his mother, for she had been diagnosed with cancer. In the course of one year, he went from being carefree to caregiver. He moved back to the French Reunion Islands where his family lived. Improbably, it was on this small volcanic island in the Indian Ocean that he was introduced to Vedanta philosophy—in French. The pain and helplessness that had suddenly shattered his life drew him to a Creole spiritual scholar who had studied Vedic Hindu thought in India. In between looking after his mother, Surya would attend the teacher's lectures and try and make sense of the questions that had begun to plague him. How do you make sense of sorrow? Why do things happen that are way beyond our control? The spiritual teachings moved him deeply, and he became the student who asked the most compelling questions.

At one point, the teacher said, 'I don't think I have all the answers you are looking for. Why don't you go to the source, the one who taught me?'

That is how Surya arrived for the first time in the land his ancestors had left behind a long time back. He went straight to the Gurukulam in Anaikatti, straight to the feet of the master. He spent a month there, sitting in on the classes, melting into that space of convergence that transcends language, culture, religion. He befriended the other students, in particular a bright-eyed young woman called Neema, because she too spoke Gujarati. She, in turn, was intrigued by this handsome French-accented, light-eyed man who had travelled across oceans to seek knowledge.

Surya wanted to stay longer, to join the teacher training course, but Dayananda Saraswati told him that this was not the right time. 'Just now, you must be with your mother,' he said, embracing him. 'I will give you the recordings of the lectures. Study every day. Write to me with any questions you have. And come back every year.'

Surya returned to the Reunion Islands, but a part of him lingered on in the Nilgiri hills. His journey home had begun.

Just as the same ragas in Hindustani music go by different names in Carnatic music, in the south, Kartikeya becomes Murugan or Subramania. This son of Shiva once lost a race around the universe to his brother Ganesha, because while Kartikeya took the competition literally, the wise little elephant-headed one simply walked around his parents. They were the universe, after all. Upset at being upstaged, Kartikeya flew away in a huff, on his peacock, to the south of India. But because he was used to living in the Himalayas, he chose to settle on a hill. This is why the Murugan temples in the south are usually perched on a hill.

The students prayed every day at the Murugan temple on the edge of the forest academy. In those days, the temple was open to the sky. There were no walls, only four pillars and a magnificent 180-degree vista of god's creation. Birds swooped in and out, and each season saw different-coloured petals flutter in like aromatic angels. The students' chants carried across the surrounding hills, which were populated by elephants and indigenous tribals.

It was in this open temple on the hill that Neema and Surya got married a few years later, in the presence of their teacher and blessed by the elements, in a ceremony that was unusual, simple and ethereal. Fire. Water. Air. Earth. Love. The couple's parents, who had arrived from Mumbai and Paris, had not experienced anything like it.

The forest academy invoked the traditional places of learning, where nature and the elements were as important to the teaching as textbooks. Subject silos were dissolved. There was a layered understanding of the universe: the plant kingdom that sustains us is not merely botany, but also divinity; the sun is a star that gives light and heat, and it is also a symbol of illumination. Psychology, cosmology, biology, literature and faith can be taught alongside, in the same curriculum, to understand life in its full splendour. There is a melding of the intellect, emotion and spiritual insight.

The natural surroundings became an extension of the classroom, and induced a sense of humility towards sentient and non-sentient beings. Ancient banyan trees stood tall with their dreadlocks spreading like endless life cycles.

During the day, peacocks strutted through the campus like entitled models. Silken spotted deer seemed totally oblivious to the two-legged creatures that had suddenly showed up, and they continued to hang around in small herds—mama deer, papa deer and many adorable baby deer. The students were advised to stay indoors after sunset because that was when wild elephants and boars roamed around freely. This was their home first.

'There were also snakes,' says Neema. 'But Swamiji told us that they are the original inhabitants of this forest and mean no harm. Leave them alone and they will leave you alone.'

He turned the snakes into ropes.

Gradually, the two rivers inside her merged into a flow of scholarship and wisdom.

I arrived at the forest academy thirty years later, welcomed by the sound of honking peacocks. The place had not changed much from the time Neema had studied there. A sign on the road outside read, 'Elephants Have Right of Way'. A hill in the distance seemed to take the shape of a resting elephant.

There was clearly a sense that we were guests of the forest and its inhabitants. Only a small part of the campus had been cleared to build the residential, dining and teaching facilities. Our rooms were depressingly decrepit. But within a day, Neema's lectures had lifted us above quotidian concerns into the high luxe of knowledge. The student had returned as the teacher, and the flow of learning continued.

We were being taught the Panchadashi, which contains the core ideas of the Upanishads. Same raga, different gharana. There is a universal consciousness. It does not get displaced. It remains the same through months, years, yugas or cycles of creation and destruction, past, present, future. It does not get involved in the day-to-day dramas of individual lives. It does not rise or set like the sun. It is self-effulgent. It has no characteristics. This underlying consciousness remains the same for everyone because if yours and mine were different, consciousness would have attributes. But it has none. It is like the hum of the cosmic tanpura, it plays before the melody begins and long after it is over.

This text, too, used the three states of waking, dreaming and deep sleep to explain consciousness. In the case of a dream, the objects are momentary and pass; in the waking state, they are relatively stable, so you can wake up to be the same person every day. But that very continuity—the same person every day—is the beguiling deception of maya, the manifest world. For, according to the Panchadashi, the waking state is no different from the dreaming state ... I had heard all this many times before, but I was not bored.

Neema explained that such an audacious idea is not so hard to trust. The one who wakes up refreshed from a deep, dreamless sleep, says, 'I know nothing, I remember nothing.' The not-knowing—the blankness—is the very object of this knowledge. Someone remained even while there was blankness. That. Is. You. It is the eternal consciousness ... A concept that is utterly mind-bogglingly wild and, frankly, I could still only assimilate it at the level of the intellect.

I began to see the value of the guru–student tradition yet again. Just as Dhondutai could never have been replaced by an online music tutorial, I could not learn Vedanta philosophy from reading books. A teacher had to break it down for me. This knowledge is so radically different from what I assumed to be true, that if I were to read about it, I would still be using my old and limited framework of comprehension. A good teacher must first make you un-know what you know, then lead you into the new understanding, using compelling imagery and examples from daily living. This was becoming my music room.

Slowly, through the process of *shravana*, or *repeated listening*, the student's feet sink slowly into the sand. Slowly, *manana*, or *contemplation*, follows and the feet sink deeper. Gradually, illumination shines forth and the salt doll begins to dissolve into the ocean. This process redirects the brain's neural pathways to observe, think and respond differently. Initially, the process requires deliberate mindfulness. Eventually, it becomes as spontaneous as breath. The salt doll's anxieties, which she was habituated to dwelling on and amplifying in her head, begin to recede. That self-absorption which had confined her is pushed back, revealing the bigger picture. The salt doll becomes one with the ocean.

There were about twenty-five of us there that December, being treated to a sliver of what our teacher had experienced so many years earlier. Our days began at 5.30 a.m. in the morning, with prayers to Dakshinamurthy, an avatar of Shiva as the first teacher in the universe. I managed to stagger out and make it at least a few times, and was rewarded by an enchanting dawn as it emerged from behind the hills.

Two elderly women, both renunciates in tangerine robes, would arrive at the temple before any of us. They always smiled kindly at me. A few days later, Surya asked if I'd like to meet them. I was wondering how I would converse with them, for I didn't speak Tamil. But I was in for a surprise. Both swaminis spoke impeccable English. Inwardly, I cringed at my presumptive bias. They had been professors of math and physics at Kolkata University and had left their jobs to serve in this ashram. What had pulled them away from their careers into this remote space, I wondered. Perhaps they realised that they weren't going to get their answers in the empirical world. Perhaps they were looking to be wise, not just clever—to know what even the eye cannot see, where neither speech goes, nor the mind, to get an inkling of what Albert Einstein called the 'mystery of the eternity of life' and the 'marvellous structure of reality', and find out that there is much more than what is perceptible. Quantum physics does after all reveal a deeply connected physical world—a way of seeing the world as a system of inseparable, interacting, harmonious components.

Perhaps they wanted to find out why the ultimate reality of Brahmn is the exact reality of the Atman.

The saplings that had been planted by the students back when Neema studied here were now tall, sheltering trees. The banyans had become immense, ancient, protective gods. In between classes, some of us would walk up a hill to the Murugan temple, which was the only place where our phones could catch 4G airwaves. The temple was now covered and complete, though perhaps less ethereal than the version in Neema's stories. There was always a peacock fluttering around it, Mr Murugan's eternal friend.

I saw a family of spotted deer a few hundred metres away, along the downward slope of the hill. They stood as still as bronze sculptures for a few moments, staring back at me. I delved into my bag to switch on my phone camera, but when I looked up again, they were gone. Were they the descendants of that mythical golden deer who was not even really a deer but an apparition that was required to move the story forward?

Before I had left for the south, I had breakfast with my sisters. My artist sister had just been on a three-week solo walk along the Narmada river, so she understood the idea of seemingly pointless excursions into the wild. My luxe sister said, 'Have a fab time,' and then added with a twinkle, 'But Namu didi, why can't you be more normal?'

It is the most loaded question of our times. What is normal? Is it the mad hatters' tea party to which we are always late? Is it a quiet interiority? Is it just being? Why has absolute knowledge moved to the fringe, while all kinds of partial or relative knowledge hog centre-stage? I thought about this as I made my way back from the eucalyptus-clad hills to a heady December in Mumbai, filled with Christmas revelry and bad traffic.

❧

Lord, make me an instrument of Your peace.
Where there is hatred, let me sow love;
Where there is injury, pardon;

Where there is doubt, faith;
Where there is despair, hope;
Where there is darkness, light;
And where there is sadness, joy.

*—St Francis of Assisi**

---

* From *The Freethinker's Prayer Book* by Khushwant Singh, published by Aleph, 2012.

RISHIKESH REDUX

I was back in the Rishikesh ashram, entering the familiar lane, next to the little tea shop that served the meltiest vegetable cheese toast. This was the place where my journey had begun, and I was back like a fluttering, seeking moth drawn to light.

It had been a few years since I was last here, and the place felt the same, and yet different. Could it be that the one who was observing had changed, not what was being observed? It was as if a mature singer was returning to the same piece of music she had learnt many years ago, with ठहराव, theheraav, a stillness within the dynamic. The notes were less hurried, the performative urge muted.

I reflexively walked towards the temple, and was delighted to see my old friend Nandi, sitting in permanent repose, wearing a hand-knitted red muffler to stay warm. He looked like a cross between a bull and a little old man. Next to Nandi was a shrine dedicated to Dayananda Saraswati. I had been told that renunciates are never cremated—they are either buried or immersed in a water body. An uncanny plaster likeness of him seemed to be looking directly into the eyes of the beholder, perhaps guiding her towards the knowledge of what is real and what is not. Many years ago, he had insisted that women have the right to read the scriptures and become teachers, challenging the severe patriarchy of the Shankaracharyas of his time. That small intervention had allowed someone like Neema to become a teacher, which, in turn, had led me to this place.

The peepul tree was dappled in the afternoon light. I could see, in its lyrical shadows, the spirits of wise men and women who had been here, giving everything else up in search of truth, seeking that which lies outside the Bermuda Triangle of power, money, relationships. They had meditated. They had learnt to recalibrate their needs. They had sought wise teachers. They had left invisible footprints.

And beyond all this, the river.

A tall man in tangerine wearing matching orange crocs and skull cap strode past us, chatting on his iPhone, and I caught the hint of a British accent. This was a newer breed of sanyasis who were arriving from all over the world. The spiritual marketplace had expanded and slyly found its way into the algorithm of worldly pursuits. There was corporate spirituality to enhance employee productivity and yoga-based spirituality for those who wanted to take the physical route; savvy self-help gurus were marketing solace for congregations filled with people struggling with their demons.

The teachers of my lineage followed a scholarly approach through the scriptures, not coloured or distorted by anyone's imagination or interpretation. Precision and nuance are essential, for it is easy to slip into inaccuracies. So often, terms like 'maya' and 'vairagya', or detachment, were lost in translation, and led to all kinds of odd behaviour.

Detachment does not mean that you push worldly things away from you; it means engaging in the world without getting entangled. Maya is not illusion; it is dependent or relative reality.

But the teachers also said that reading the texts, or mugging up Vedic chants, would not make you a wise person. It is only the beginning. Repetition. Contemplation. Practice. Repetition. Contemplation. Practice. And finally, grace. That's when the river takes over and the salt doll dissolves in the water, after which there are no more questions.

The river was the closest I would come to touching eternity.

It was comforting to be back here and meet familiar faces, as well as some new ones. I felt oddly at home in this place of learning. I knew that the simple amenities belied the seven-star sophistication of what was on offer. The ashram turns many things inside out. I was now truly a spiritual archaeologist trying to unearth a philosophy hidden like shaligrams in the river.

This year, there were some unusual looking young foreigners roaming around the ashram. They looked like hippies from Woodstock, except that there was an intensity in their eyes that did not seem to be induced by a smoky stimulant. They spent a lot of time praying in the temple, chanting in Sanskrit with astonishing precision.

The group was from Brazil, and was visiting India with their teacher, Jonas Masetti, an impish young man who wore a peacock feather in his hat. This Portuguese-speaking mechanical engineer had been a successful finance professional in Sao Paulo, but one day, he decided to leave it all to become a teacher of Vedanta. Later, he would tell us how he found his teacher Gloria, how he found India, and how he found himself.

During these retreats, every evening after dinner, we would sit around for a more informal satsang, where people shared their expertise or their sorrow, or sang. These sessions often concluded with a few of us boisterously singing old Hindi film songs. I noticed that Neema loved this and joined in heartily. 'You don't have to box yourself into being this or that (when "you are that"!),' she once joked. A few days later, we had a joint satsang with the Brazilians, and Jonas told us his story, again making it clear that boundaries exist only on maps. The world is more fluid and connected than we can possibly imagine. Can a river tell when it is entering another country? Do flamingos need visas?

'I started my journey to deal with an underlying sadness that just wouldn't go away,' said Jonas. 'I used to see how even the most successful people around me were stressed, depressed, taking sleeping pills ... It didn't make sense. So, that's how I started. I stayed on the journey because it was so interesting. I had never heard anything like this.' He paused, and I saw tears rolling down his cheeks. 'Then, there was transformation. Moulting. Magic.'

Jonas now runs a centre of learning in the hills of Petropolis, near Rio de Janeiro, where he teaches the Upanishads and the Bhagavad Gita. His students—young professionals, homemakers, yoga teachers—were not trying to become Hindu, whatever that elusive term means, but were embarking on a study of the self. Their teacher told them that this knowledge would help them understand themselves and thereby help them lead a happier and more harmonious life.

After addressing us, Jonas pulled out a Brazilian drum and sang a song of the Amazon. Some others joined in. The singing was hypnotic, a jungle chant that seemed to be infused with the cries of toucans and the gait of spider monkeys. We sat there mesmerised, as if we were being coiled into some other plane. Suddenly, we heard a drumroll outside. It was an unexpected cloudburst, not typical for that time of year. I looked out and saw a blurry moon through the pelting rain. I think most of us in that room were moved by some sense of the intangible forces that drive the universe. And those who had inhaled the peace pipes of the rainforest knew that there was nothing more to know.

In every retreat, we studied an Upanishad in the morning class, and the complementary chapter from the Bhagavad Gita in the afternoon. They both contain the same core ideas; the Upanishad is more abstract, while the Gita translates that knowledge into a toolkit for living.

This year, for the first time, I started understanding the magic of the Gita. I had always heard that this book was important, but I scarcely knew much beyond the basics, that you must do your dharma, your duty; that you must perform actions without focusing on the results. I didn't know that it contained a practical guide to living and was imbued with grace that could, as a shloka goes, make the mute one sing and the lame one scale a mountain. I was astounded by the stories of how a minute action can trigger colossal outcomes, like the butterfly that flaps its wings and triggers a typhoon in another part of the world. The Gita is never prescriptive or moralistic, it lays out possibilities; these nudge you to navigate wisely.

This year, we were studying Chapter Thirteen, in which Krishna lays out qualities of the mind that prepare the seeker for the knowledge of the self, the truth. In particular, these nine values continue to help me eject conditioned beliefs and dislodge old patterns from my mind.

- Absence of self-conceit: Eliminating the exaggerated self-respect that we all unwittingly seek. If you are comfortable in your skin, and secure about your accomplishments, you need not care how others view you. Your abilities speak for themselves, just as a tree bursts into flowers without proclaiming that it has. Besides, so many seen and unseen circumstances contribute to your achievements—not just your birth, but also the man who drove the train that took you to work, the sun that enables photosynthesis to give you food, it doesn't stop ... And it seems faulty and foolish to take too much credit.
- Accommodation: Cheerful acceptance of that which one cannot change in a person or a situation. Just as I might want someone to change to suit my preferences, that person would likely want the same from me. We accept things or creatures just as they are, whether it is a blazing hot sun on a summer afternoon or a bird that poos on one's head, so why not apply the

same logic to one another. One way to achieve this mindset is to follow the deterministic view that offers the back story that triggered a behaviour or situation, why a person burst into a fit of rage or cruelty. It is the capacity to separate the person from the action.

The Stoics talk about Amor Fati. Embracing what is, not passively but mindfully, with compassion not judgement, and with an attitude that views everything as curriculum for growth. This also blends into the famous serenity prayer for alcoholics and their co-dependents: Lord, grant me the serenity to accept the things I cannot change, the courage to change the things I can, and the wisdom to know the difference.

- Alignment of thought, speech and action: Mahatma Gandhi famously said, 'Always aim at complete harmony of thought and word and deed.' This liberates the mind from trying to cover up any pretence or dissonance.
- Cultivating objective dispassion towards objects that we experience through our sense organs: Enjoying each one, but not getting compulsively tangled up in them. There are two words in the language of Vedanta: 'raga' and 'dvesa'. For the first time, I understood raga to mean something other than an arrangement of musical notes. Raga means craving. A dispassionate mind sees objects clearly, for what they are, without imputing extra value—therefore anxiety—to them. So, you enjoy a relationship without getting embroiled in it; you appreciate abundance but are not insecure about it going away.

- Equanimity: This is the capacity to accept results that are desirable as well as those that are not. It is the mind's ability to be neither too elated nor too dejected. If something doesn't go my way, I must approach life with a calm objectivity and do what has to be done. Things get muddled up when we project our bias or emotional response on to a situation that is unfolding. I thought about various moments in my life when this understanding could have been applied and so much drama averted. Could this practical approach of complete acceptance, followed by solution-oriented behaviour, be some ancient version of cognitive behavioural therapy?
- Prasada buddhi: When you go into a place of worship, you may be given a rotting banana or a delicious mango. You don't turn your nose up at it, because it is a blessing. By extension, everything in life is a blessing that comes through the will of god. Therefore, gracefully accept all results—of one's own actions or others' actions—as blessings. They stem from the infallible laws of the universe.

Krishna says in the Bhagavad Gita: 'If there is unswerving devotion to me, seeing nothing other than me as the giver of results, naturally there will be sameness of mind, for favourable and unfavourable results.'*

---

* From *Srimad Bhagavad Gita*, translated by Swami Dayananda Saraswati and published by Arsha Vidya Research and Publication Trust, 2007.

- Affection without obsession: This is the ability to care without becoming obsessed or feeling possessive or too attached. Don't claim anyone, whether son, husband, parent, even a close friend. It's a delicate balance you have to achieve as a mother, to facilitate the best for your child but also give him a sense of autonomy to fall, rise and learn.
- A love for solitude: I had this escapist cousin who would keep travelling, and one day his disgruntled wife said to him, 'Darling, you keep running away, but remember you are taking yourself with you!' You cannot, after all, escape yourself. Befriending solitude allows the mind to declutter, to be able to move towards knowledge of the self, the creator and all creation.
- Mastery over the mind: What an incredible superpower!

I learnt that these values laid out by Krishna, the charioteer of our lives, when assimilated, can help us overcome obstacles and stride with clarity and conviction. And, with this new inner compass, I decided I was going to create new neural pathways, scenic diversions from the highways of habitual thinking.

Coincidences are destiny's tiny miracles winking at you. One such wink was that my birthday fell in the middle of Neema's December retreats. This year I was turning fifty-four. I had managed to avert a scary surprise party that my sisters were plotting in Mumbai, and was happy to be in my happy place. Instead of champagne on ice, I received an unusual gift. Neema and Surya chanted the entire Bhagavad Gita for me—eighteen chapters, two-and-a-half hours—under the gaze of the gods and Swamiji. I had finally turned the pages of the great book which, many years ago, had inspired my grandparents to name their first two children Bhagwat and Gita. My father is the B in the BG.

The students threw a birthday party for me in the ashram dining hall with spiced cookies from a local biscuit seller. They sang Happy Birthday in seven different languages—Russian, Kannada, Hindi, Portuguese, German, Flemish and Marathi. I felt grateful and loved.

Later that evening, when the sky draped itself in an indigo silk robe with the confidence of a tzar, we sat together near the river, and my teachers chanted the Rudram, a Vedic chant praising the all-powerful Shiva. It always left me feeling something, though I was still not sure what. But something very new, for sure—maybe it was unconditional love, safety.

Afterwards, Shona and I sat facing the water in silence, watching people strike a match and send their tremulous little prayers floating down the water: make my child pass her exams; make my father feel better soon; let our mustard crop be healthy this year; help me on the path to eternal bliss.

I turned to my friend, my sakhi.

'How lucky I am that you pushed me to come here, even though I was initially so cynical. Thank you, friend. I owe you!'

'No, Namu, you don't! You have no idea how much you helped me with contour maps when we were in the seventh grade. Don't you remember? The night before the geography exam when I thought I was going to fail?'

We laughed at the memory of those traumatic school days. We both knew that ripples are created even when a pebble has not been tossed into the water. One friend was silently telling another: if I knew the way, I would take you home.

❧

Ripple in still water
When there is no pebble tossed
Nor wind to blow

Reach out your hand, if your cup be empty
If your cup is full, may it be again
Let it be known there is a fountain
That was not made by the hands of men

– From 'Ripple' by Grateful Dead

ALMOST SANYASA

A WORLDLY RENUNCIATE

Who is a wise person?

A sanyasi, or renunciate, because she takes just as much food as she needs, does not hoard pointlessly, and is comfortable in any environment. She is free. Her focus is the path to enlightenment. She is like the frangipani which intuitively ends up leaning towards the sun no matter which way you turn it.

I was now befriending the inevitable.

THE ARROGANT YOGINI

The ego is a strange thing. It always needs something to attach itself to, like a monkey needs a branch to hang from, even though that branch could break and fall any time. Some pick the branch of wealth; others of intellect. The ego is that part of our 'I-self' which makes us believe that our individual mind-body is solely responsible for a particular outcome.

The ego of the spiritual seeker is particularly hideous, insidious. It can be even worse than the inflated ego of the wealthy man or the brilliant musician, for all it does is simply replace the vanity of riches or talent with spiritual superiority, and it is disguised in white robes.

As I sank my feet deeper into these sands, two things started happening to me, which were a little off-kilter, and definitely irksome for those close to me. The first was that, because I had tasted the magic potion, I started to feel like I was in some way privileged. I would talk ceaselessly about the Upanishads and how amazing they are, even around folks who were uninterested or didn't share my view. I impatiently interrupted those who didn't understand what I was saying. Some of my rationalist friends, especially my journalist colleagues, would roll their eyes as I babbled breathlessly about god stuff. I think my poor son got the worst of it because he was my captive audience. I would bore him to sleep because, in the early days, these new ideas consumed me. I think he started fearing that I had turned into a hellishly right-wing mom. He was also embarrassed, given that many strange ideas were being unleashed in the country in the name of Hinduism. One day, he said, 'Mom, why can't you live this teaching quietly instead of preaching about it!'

I have always been the school head girl who went slightly rogue. I have to constantly watch myself to ensure I don't go from being arrogant to spiritually arrogant. But life always manages to bring you down to earth. There is a story in the Keno Upanishad in which even the devas, or gods, are shown as not immune to the superiority problem.

The gods were feeling chuffed about winning a battle, and forgot to acknowledge that there was a higher power that existed beyond even them. They were proudly claiming glory and 'doership', that dangerous delusion which precedes a downfall. Then, a spirit appeared before them.

First, Agni, the god of fire, went to find out who this exalted being was. When the spirit asked him to identify himself, he replied like a brazen Delhi-ite might, 'Don't you know who I am? I am the powerful Agni, and I can burn anything on this earth.'

The spirit asked, can you burn this blade of grass? Agni tried and tried, but the grass did not burn.

Next, Vayu, the god of wind, arrived. Again, when asked who he was, he proudly proclaimed that he was the god who could blow anything away. When the blade of grass was put before him, he huffed and he puffed, but it did not move. He slunk away like his predecessor had.

Finally, the king of the gods, Indra, was sent to find out who this spirit was. At that moment, the spirit disappeared and in its place Uma, Shiva's lovely consort, his Shakti, appeared.

Shiva Shakti encompasses all that there is, past-present-future, manifest and unmanifest. Glory belongs only to that higher spirit. All beings—whether the most exceptional scientist or musician or billionaire—are instruments of 'thy will'. Ramakrishna says in *The Gospel*: 'The water from the roof flows through a spout that is shaped like a lion's head. It looks as if the lion were bringing the water out through its mouth. But look at the source of the water! A cloud gathers in the sky, and rain falls on the roof; then the water flows through the pipe, and at last comes out through the spout.'

One of the many things I learnt from my music teacher, in between the ragas, was the tea lesson.

'You think you're making the tea, eh?' she chuckled, pulling out her little brass vessels.

'Don't ever forget that someone far away cropped the tea leaves; another milked a cow; someone pressed sugar out of the cane … Oh, and remember the sun that made it all possible, and also thank the water and the fire that came together to give you this comforting cup of chai. There are so many seen and unseen factors, known and unknown, which enable every little action and achievement. Those unheard notes are as important as those you hear.'

She also told me about how, behind every great artiste, there is an invisible backdrop of people without whom they may not have achieved greatness. When her teacher Bhurji Khan fell severely ill, her uncle, a doctor, worked relentlessly to heal him just so that his niece could get a few more years of training.

I began to understand the role of different elements in my life—the employee who cleans my flat every morning allows me to focus on my work; the anonymous labourers who built my apartment building so many years ago, brick by brick, gave me my home; the gulmohar tree my neighbour had planted has grown to the third floor, turning my room into a treehouse ... No one person or experience is more important than another. All are needed for the world to exist. The writer will write. The farmer will farm. The chanter will chant. The muezzin will call to prayer. The liver will live. The sun shines on all, unconditionally.

But organised religion often goes against the very essence of the faith's teachings. It becomes organised arrogance. I shudder to see so many Hindus believe that they are better than everyone else, that they have all the answers, that saffron—or my tangerine—is the best colour in the spectrum of faith. The stratifying politics of the human mind has entered that which is beyond the human. In iconography across the country, the noble Rama has been turned into a pastiche of a hero figure who has to vanquish some perceived enemy; he has to protect faith as if it is property. Can you protect a universal, timeless vibration? From what? From whom? It does not make sense to me because the wisdom of the sages reveals itself again and again through the ages. And that wisdom is beyond man.

The second thing that has started happening—and it has been mildly unnerving—is that I cannot relate to many of the things that once excited me. I see dramatic edifices crumbling in slow motion, including ideas about education, role models, the meaning of success.

I have begun to see how everyone's quest is essentially the same: a search for happiness. Some clutch status symbols like a big fat wedding, while others aspire for literary recognition. A degree from Princeton has become the intellectual version of a Prada purse; both brands have masterfully conjured delusions of superiority. Does a professor of history know how to grow rice? Why is one deemed more important than the other?

The art market is not that different from the stock market, with off-the-chart prices pushed by canny peddlers under an acrylic veneer of pretension. Some in the world of ideas spout lofty ideals about freedom and equality, but regularly exclude and reject those who don't agree with them. People who outrage about the caste system often practise their own intellectual hierarchies. Rationalists scoff at faith, uncaring that prayer may be the only way some people know to step out of themselves.

How does any form of othering qualify a person as liberal?

Can kindness be conditional?

Why has faith become the opposite of reason?

The absence of humility, the inability to see that everyone has their place in the world, is one of the most unattractive aspects of the current binary discourse.

I sometimes feel like Holden Caulfield, the wry and wonderful character in *Catcher in the Rye*, to whom everything seems 'phony'. It didn't surprise me at all to discover that his creator, J.D. Salinger, had been influenced by the teachings of the crazy-cool Thakur of Dakshineswar. Back in the sixties, Salinger had started spending time in a building on East 94th St in Manhattan: the Ramakrishna–Vivekananda Centre. He spent many years in solitude in New Hampshire. Perhaps he was grappling with the idea of his own authorship. Perhaps he was aware that even the most creative writer could never compete with the Great Author.

❧

Yogananda writes in his *Autobiography of a Yogi* that one of the unwritten rules for the spiritual seeker is patience. Nandi the bull is the eternally patient devotee who sits at every Shiva temple. At some point, I went and bought a stone Nandi in Chor Bazaar, Mumbai's oldest flea market, and placed it at the entrance to my home in Alibag. It was a reminder that I must be patient in my quest.

Repose is also a reminder that while things are constantly happening around me—good and bad, pleasant and unpleasant—I should know that there is also, simultaneously, an unchanging state of pure meditative silence that remains unaffected. These states are not in opposition. They have been translated symbolically into Shiva and Shakti, Eternity and Energy, famously captured in the dancing Nataraja found in every antique shop in India—where the figure of Shiva is both dynamic and still.

There is enormous power in maya or shakti, the manifest universe, but you also have the power to see through it. Knowing that makes you live a little differently. The ego retreats because you know it is a mere construct based on factors that are constantly changing—your body, your position at work, your faculties. When broken down, arguments take place between one ego construct and another, both of which have a limited or disjointed view of things, while the 'is' of life carries on, based on factors way beyond anyone's control.

I am learning to be the two wise birds on that apocryphal branch, participating as well as observing. I do what I have to do, but like a stage actor, without getting stuck in the role, nor desperate for a given outcome. The young athlete who plays rugby with feral ferocity can also grow into a wise adult who plays the game with passion and detachment.

My son often argued with me. 'With this comatose approach, there would be no revolutionary movements, Mum. We'd still be hanging people from trees.'

'Do whatever is in your sphere of influence,' the mothership replied. 'But also know that there is a much bigger picture that is playing out many, *many* variables that will impact the outcome.'

Everything is a consequence of something, I explained to him. Recognising that nothing is separate from its antecedents nor its future results helps cultivate an objective approach to what is unfolding in the present moment. Such knowledge keeps you in balance. It helps you to not lose your temper over traffic or politics. You get the scent of the flower that once bloomed and the mud about to be drenched by rain. You hear the pain of those who don't cry out. You tune into the roar of silence.

This holds true for individuals, for societies, for nations, until you bow to the ultimate causeless cause, and there are no more questions to be answered.

'So, do we have free will?' C and I often had the debate—the physics student and the student of Vedanta.

'It eternally confounds me, son. But yes, I believe we do—partially.'

The Yoga Vasishtha sums it up as follows: 'Self-effort is of two categories—that of past births (what we call fate or karma) and that of this birth. The latter effectively counteracts the former. Fate is nothing but self-effort from a past incarnation. There is constant conflict between these two in this life, and that which is more powerful triumphs.'

Neema used to explain that the human being is privileged with the capacity to make choices. When your choice aligns with the nuanced and contextual laws of dharma, you get equitable consequences. And life has a feedback mechanism. So, you know. You just know.

This is how we can mindfully alter our destiny.

In the end, the eternal, in which nothing happens, and the phenomenal world of maya, in which things are seemingly happening and being experienced by our individuated selves, are one. Both are true. The microscope and the telescope eventually reveal the same thing. This paradox translates into the most important equation in Vedic thought, the equation between Brahmn and Atman, the eternal self and the Namita self.

I am that.

That I am.

Tat tvam asi.

WHEN DESTRUCTION IS DIVINE

On this journey that I was on, there was one aspect that I was still not able to connect with. Why does one go to a temple? Why can't we pray in the quiet of our hearts? In fact, what is the need for any formal prayers? I didn't quite agree with how organised religion had inflicted itself on a purer spirituality which respects other faiths, seeks unity, and is not located in any single culture or historical context.

Praying and temple-hopping seem to be India's national pastimes, but I couldn't relate to the practice and politics of active worship, especially because there were all kinds of spurious rules of exclusion. I once trekked up to the ancient Kankeshwar temple in Alibag with a friend. We were enchanted by the walk up the stone steps and the little shrines that popped up like mellow mushrooms along the way. Just before we reached the top of the hill, we stumbled upon a Brahmakund, a water body configured like a Mandala, with steps on all sides. It was so silent, we could almost hear a spider spinning its daydreams. Its web dangled from a twig, intact and perfect. I had never seen something so delicate, so nearly invisible.

At the temple, a priest with crooked teeth asked my friend if she was Hindu. Taken by surprise, she innocently answered, 'Syrian Christian.' He didn't let her enter. Really? There are conditions in the House of God? I was ashamed of this inhospitable ending to a beautiful morning.

So, where does prayer fit in this estrangement between religion and spirituality?

My observations of those who prayed did little to convince me either. My grandparents would often be gossiping while performing rituals. The workers in our home prayed in front of colourful calendar pictures of gods who looked like film stars. My music teacher used to conduct an elaborate daily ritual of bathing and dressing each of the figurines in her doll's-house altar, which I found more fascinating, as a child anthropologist might, than edifying. We all participated in festivals like Ganesha Chaturthi and Diwali, but I remember the fun and the food rather than the prayers.

But there were times—and I believe every person goes through this—when I felt such trenchant hopelessness that I mentally dropped to my knees and reached for an invisible analgesic.

Neema always says that prayer is the most effective and efficient use of one's free will. After you've tried everything to change or improve a situation, prayer is the final variable, as you turn helpless vulnerability into constructive surrender. When I chatted with my friend Shona about my scepticism, she simply said: 'Prayer has a lot of power. Just experience it.' She made it sound as matter-of-fact as 'a cup of tea makes you feel good'.

Hinduism believes in intangible forces, beyond what is available to human perception and intellect, and prayer is a way of connecting with that idea. It's like knowing that we charge our phones from the electric lines which in turn get charged by the power grid. Prayer taps into that power which charges the universe.

Being a compulsively proactive personality type, I shrugged off doubts and started praying—not the way I used to earlier, those occasional transactional conversations with my kandy-koloured gods, asking for this or that, or a bedtime prayer as a teenager, imploring that my crush object reciprocate my feelings and, later, a prayer to ensure that my son stayed well. Sometimes, my prayer would just be a 'thank you' for some unexpected triumph. For the longest time, I prayed that my family be whole and healed.

But this was the first time I was getting into formal worship. I created an altar from a tray with colourful lotus patterns made by children from a non-profit organisation, Akanksha, in which I placed a random assortment of sweet little statues and pictures of gods and goddesses I had collected from here there and everywhere: a silver Ganesha given to me by Dhondutai; several Shivas and Nandis in stone and brass; a picture of Mahalaxmi from Kolhapur and one of Zarathustra from a shop near the fire temple in Kalbadevi; an icon of Christ bought on a trip to Cyprus; a psychedelic Guru Nanak painted by a friend and a clay Durga from Kolkata, all hanging out together, a full United Nations of benevolence. There was one important absence, though. In deference to my longstanding Amar Akbar Anthony loyalty, I needed an Islamic god in there, so I added a small bust of Alladiya Khan. He may not have been a *God* god, but he was my god of music. On the wall, I hung an unusual old portrait of Shiva reaching out to Parvati in a moment that captures his vulnerability and her strength. Shiva Shakti. Please, dear god, I also want some of that.

I lit organic agarwood incense every morning, and prayed. Most of the time, I asked for alignment to the higher order because I had begun to realise that I didn't know what was best for me. How many times had I read, be careful what you wish for because it might come true. It may be for your good that your prayer is not granted!

I also started learning the Rudram, a powerful Vedic chant that came into my life as a murmur and grew into an inner opera.

In the twilight hour in Rishikesh, when the sky turns inky and the moon throws its silvery tint on the water, the reflection of a reflection, we walk down the stone steps to a flat spot by the river. We lay down mats and sit on them, around our teachers, the centrifugal force. Neema and Surya then recite the Rudram, their gently strident male and female voices a comingled duet against the background score of the river's roar. The freezing cold is countered by the warmth of sweet devotion.

This had become an annual ritual. With every passing year, I started recognising certain words, or anticipating the change in metre. By the end of the chant, about twenty minutes long, I think most of us experienced a sense of annihilation as well as wholeness; the two were not mutually antagonistic.

I was blown. I wanted to understand why this ode to Shiva was so impactful. Who is this gorgeous and terrifying god with matted hair who danced the dance of destruction? How does he consume everything, playing his game of time, juggling the sun and the moon like balls in the air? Why is he surrounded by hideous, imperfect creatures? How does he embrace all with the unflappable serenity of a yogi? It took several years, but it came to me, not like a lightning bolt, but more gradually, the way a lotus blooms.

Rudra means the one who makes you cry. Rudra also means the one who takes away pain. Suddenly, this apparent paradox made sense. He is the all. What we term the good or the bad, right or wrong, the everything that is here, creation as well as destruction, even that which we think—from our limited human perspective—is terrible or unfair. He/she/they is/are the All.

The Rudram has changed my relationship with the idea of destruction and dissolution. I began to understand that life—and the universe—is in perpetual motion, and what we view as 'destruction' is merely one of the midway reels in a never-ending, circular story. We just don't know where it ends or begins.

It is true, of course, that there is destruction happening all the time: every present moment has to be destroyed for a new one to emerge in its fullness. Imagine if all past and present moments were jumbled together, the result could be like a bad acid trip! Inside our bodies, old cells are constantly self-destructing for new ones to form. The destruction of fear allows us to plunge into the unknown. The destruction of hubris leaves space for humility. A dead tree ends up as the nutritious mulch for emerging plants. The universe is dynamic and intelligent. Many organisms that have lived on this planet are gone forever because their time was up in the ecosystem. Nature is a great leveller.

Everything is evanescent, so destruction is critical and inevitable. You cannot taxidermise a moment. Nor can you freeze a stage of life unless you turn into a wax statue. Yet, we habitually try to hold on to moments, people, our youth, and life itself. When any of these are destroyed, even the most intelligent among us have tantrums like a toddler whose lollipop has been snatched away.

People die, entire civilisations get destroyed, planets explode. But that would be from the human eye's perspective. The timelines are very different in the Hindu scriptures where thousands of yugas collapse into one Brahma day.

In the dynamic dance of Shiva as Nataraja, all forms are but changing expressions of the singular consciousness or Brahmn. Everything exists as potential before it manifests, plays out its role in the universe, and then resolves back into that undifferentiated energy. There is a seeming statis amidst constant, thunderous movement. Nataraja remains eternally poised in the midst of his cosmic dance. The circle of flames surrounding him represents the energy of the universe; creation and destruction are happening simultaneously while his expression is one of complete equanimity, the abiding spectator.

Destruction can be good. It has its place. I knew that, to become wise, my ignorance had to be destroyed.

After the fourth year of listening to the Rudram in that sacred spot, I knew I wanted to learn it—as a prayer, but also as a challenge to help turbocharge my fraying brain cells and fuel the engine of memory. Honestly, I could have been learning Italian or embroidery, but learning an ancient Vedic chant seemed more interesting, extraordinary. And then the universe winked at me again.

That December, the day I returned to Mumbai from Rishikesh, a message popped up in my inbox announcing an online course on the Rudram by a woman called Shantala. Originally a software engineer from Bangalore, she now lived in a Belgian village with her Flemish husband and children, and taught Vedic chants.

This was yet another journey into the unknown, and different from anything I had done before, but I had begun to pay heed to my inner voice, allowing it to mentor me, undistracted by any other chatter. I started reading up about these chants and learnt that, like sunshine and millets, Vedic chants impact our metabolism. In 2008, UNESCO inscribed this oral tradition into its list that compiled humanity's intangible cultural heritage, along with the Palestinian Hikaye women's storytelling practice, a carnival tradition in Belgium, and other old forms of expression.

Vedic chants are revealed wisdom. They come to wise people after they have vacuumed their minds of chatter and created an inner environment that is conducive to receiving. They contain the truth of the universe. A truth that was always there, like gravity. No scientist invented gravity. But one did prepare himself for years so that when the apple fell, he could access the insight.

The wisdom behind the chants has been meticulously coded into sound and can be broken into metre, enunciation and words, all of these being equally important for the vibrational end game. The chants rise and fall in a rhythmic cadence, like a horse trot, or the rain, to enable memorisation. If the pronunciation is not precise, the meaning may alter. When one hears the mutilated version of chants blaring on ringer tones, it can be as unnerving as finding a Palaeolithic rock-cut cave painted purple or suddenly hearing a nishad note in raga Bhoop.

Listening to a bored priest chant the Rudram in a mechanical manner did not interest me. I was told that you have to absorb the meaning and ask Shiva for what you want from the innermost space in your heart. I was fortunate that the meanings have been translated and explained in simple English by Dayananda Saraswati in a book with a blue cover that lies by my bedside, along with another little blue book by Pico Iyer, *The Art of Stillness*. I started paying attention to the meaning of the chant: which is that, essentially, everything is divinity. Imputing value judgements of good or bad, right or wrong, are from a human perspective.

The electric combination of precise recitation with clear comprehension can be a game changer. I feel that it has begun to transform my relationship with myself and with the constantly changing universe. I am also learning the art of stillness, to pause when habitual thoughts generating habitual anxieties come knocking. It can be a superpower that helps dislodge the connection between an external event and one's response to it, making the two independent of each other.

The Rudram is essentially a long-drawn composition to praise and placate the angry, weapon-wielding Rudra—who makes you cry—into the benign Shiva who redirects his weapons to destroy your inner demons. It is a prayer to turn an aggressive, destructive god into his meditative form, negative into positive. The Rudram neutralises your past karma to enable a life of happiness that is free of disease. It dissipates the obstacles that come in the way of achieving your goals. All this might sound like spiritual babble, but the underlying philosophy is monumentally expansive and liberal.

Here is why: in most chants, you are invoking some divine aspect of a particular deity, which is the personification of a particular characteristic. Ganesha for wisdom and luck, Lakshmi for prosperity, Saraswati for knowledge. When you turn to Rudra, to Shiva, you can no longer choose only the good things. You are accepting the reality that everything is divinity, whether it is good or bad, kind or mean, living or non-living. The prayer captures divine oneness in all its infinite manifestations.

Being a writer, I find the words of the chant immensely colourful and imaginative. For, the chant praises everything there is, from humans to goats, green leaves, dead leaves, dry leaves, good people, thieves, even 'clever thieves' (now, that's truly inclusive!), rain, lightning, the prana or life force of every animal and plant, still water, gushing streams, sound as well as the echo of the sound ... It goes on and on, covering everything that exists in the manifest universe. There is no distinction between desirable and undesirable, much like the German psychologist Carl Jung inviting people to befriend their shadow selves. All that is here is divinity. The seemingly antagonistic forces of creativity and destruction are in unity. Everything is manifest in its unique separateness, but is also simultaneously the undifferentiated absolute.

How extraordinary that everything is changing or has the potential to change. A good guy can become bad and a bad guy can suddenly turn around and write an entire epic; this is possibly why some countries have decided to call prisons correctional facilities rather than jails.

This potential mutability brings about a certain objective understanding and, therefore, acceptance—that no one is entirely good or bad, although an action can be good or bad and will accordingly invite consequence. But everything is unfolding exactly as it is meant to. Accept every person, event, situation, and then invite the wisdom to navigate it, to draw the correct boundaries, with compassion and insight. What evidence is there that the ideas folded into the Rudram are believable? The proof is only experiential.

I often shut my eyes and sit in that space by the Ganga, listening to the chanting and the river, even when I am not there. It is like having a live painting that you can step into, like Mary Poppins did with Bert, to be part of their fantasy carnival, and then everything is mostly okay.

I now pray every morning in front of my multicultural altar, some might say like a little old lady, sometimes fervently, sometimes quietly. It has become a daily ritual. There was a time when I would feel cringey or apologetic and embarrassed to admit this. But as I lean into my authenticity, not squeezing myself into some phantom expectations of myself, all I can say is that it makes me peaceful. I have observed myself moulting from arrogance to helplessness to vulnerability to humility to beautiful surrender, where surrender is not defeat but a long exhalation after years of short, hurried breaths.

By the way, one of the secrets about Shiva is that he has a blind spot for his devotees. Blessings will be showered like a heady monsoon on the one who chants his name, whether he is a mean-spirited ten-headed demon or a woman from South Mumbai trying to make sense of life.

Stupid ones, smart ones, learned ones
—All are crazy for You.
But none of them grasp You
They'd stew in hell
Meanwhile, the lame one crosses the mountain.
The deaf-mute echoes You
The sinner attains grace.
The wicked one ceases to harm.
Says Tuka,
He is everywhere
He plays the game
*He watches from a distance**

* From *Says Tuka*, translated from the Marathi by Dilip Chitre and published by Penguin Books India, 1991.

OLD PICTURE, NEW LENS

I had begun to feel more secure within, trusting some invisible force that was leading me exactly where I was supposed to go. I just had to follow the mantra to keep walking. I didn't even want any predictions about my future because I had begun to feel that the process is the goal. Besides, a little suspense is fun. I was scripting my own mystery mini-series.

P and I tried to get divorced again, this time with another lawyer representing us because the earlier one had stopped taking our calls. We sent in our papers, including a very faded marriage certificate with the signatures barely legible, maybe because it had been photocopied so many times. But just then, COVID unleashed its madness, the world came to a standstill, and that was that.

My ma-in-law used to say in her strong Sindhi accent, '*Is mein bhi koyi raaz.*' There is always a hidden reason for why things happen, or don't happen.

When an unprecedented circumstance strikes your life, you are forced to move away from the robotic programming that seemed to work earlier. Two years of on-off lockdowns had a different impact on different people. Those who could not handle life without the endless props of distraction fell apart. Those who secretly craved an excuse to guiltlessly avoid those distractions became serene. I found myself becoming more still and, in an odd paradox, felt more alive.

The kaleidoscope moves. Same pixels, different picture. It's like discovering music in what you thought was silence. You listen with your eyes, and see with your ears. You suddenly pay attention to your breath, to the wind, to the sound of crickets, and to the unstruck note. You roll into the contemplative mind.

I feel like I am moulting, peeling off the pleasant patina that had long been my sheath against … myself! I didn't want to be fenced in by any of my identities. I was all of them and yet they didn't define me. I took a deep breath and changed my Instagram bio to: 'I am that', although fully aware that it might mystify and baffle many who knew me, maybe even elicit a sneer or two. Well, hello again. Pleased to meet you, hope you guess my name.

It's like the numbered lenses the optometrist places on your trial glasses that suddenly make you see the letters clearly. These wisdom-tinted lenses have taken me beyond my seeing eyes into understanding the subterranean mysteries of life, that hidden language with which ants communicate with one another and the not-really-blue sky spreads across the world. The lenses are also panoramic. They help me see not just the waves that appear in my line of vision; they give me a sense of the ocean that contains all waves, big small bad good past present future.

I am also learning to navigate life differently, blowing like a light breeze, flowing like water. I am immersed in the experience, not thinking about whether it is pleasant or unpleasant. I am trying to observe without judgement. Neutrality can be an enormous superpower, for it enables you to interact with what is, not what should be or could be, neither forcing nor manipulating an outcome. It has not made me passive. In fact, it has made me more actively engaged, as mother, friend, journalist, citizen, but with quiet detachment, knowing that everything is happening exactly as it is meant to, authored by a force well beyond me. My thoughts and actions are being driven by this new wisdom, though old habits and hobbies keep shadowing me, and I have to gently request them to find other pastures. Slowly, slowly. It's a process, but the journey is becoming the destination.

In any case, I know I am a tiny participant in a vast, all-inclusive and highly intelligent universe. It is one in which, no matter what happens, the sun rises every morning and the tides continue their incantatory chant. And nature periodically throws down a lavender chiffon twilight that makes you gasp and surrender, even if momentarily. I am a drop in this incredible flow. So many before me have danced to the beat of this knowledge and so many more will.

All this existed long before me, and will continue to flourish long after I have vanished, both physically and as a gentle memory. I may become the mud that one day nurtures a giant banyan or offers sustenance to an army of industrious ants. Or, I might be one of those ants. Or star dust.

Those who were worried or weirded out by my walk into the wild side are now chastened because, outwardly, nothing in my life has really changed. I am the same person, sometimes serious, sometimes goofy, sometimes unabashedly covetous, other times downright earthy, lying on the grass and gazing at a kind-hearted moon. Silently thankful. Perhaps what's puzzling you is the nature of my game?

I think I am turning into a worldly renunciate. When you know who you really are, then it is that much easier to play all the roles that are expected of you. The actor is neither the princess nor the beggar that the script demands her to be. I can retreat into my inner room—not the music room, but my own, very private, very sacred ashram strewn with tangerine-coloured marigolds that are invisible to the eye, visible to the heart. I am returning to the lap of a grandmother who exuded the aroma of ghee and safety, returning to an unconditional space. It is a cyclical homecoming that somehow connects past, present and, hopefully, future.

It was at the end of the second lockdown—a time when time stood still—that I also saw two goldfish being still for the first time, no longer two lost souls swimming in a fish bowl, year after year. P and I reconnected as old friends and seekers, transcending the playdough roles of husband and wife. We are still married, but live in different homes, separated by water.

I sometimes wonder if that is what Krishna meant—
Among other things—or one way of putting the same thing:
That the future is a faded song, a Royal Rose or a lavender spray
Of wistful regret for those who are not yet here to regret,
Pressed between yellow leaves of a book that has never been opened.
And the way up is the way down, the way forward is the way back.

*– T.S. Eliot**

* From 'The Dry Salvages' by T.S. Eliot, https://stuff.mit.edu/people/dpolicar/writing/poetry/poems/fareForward.html.

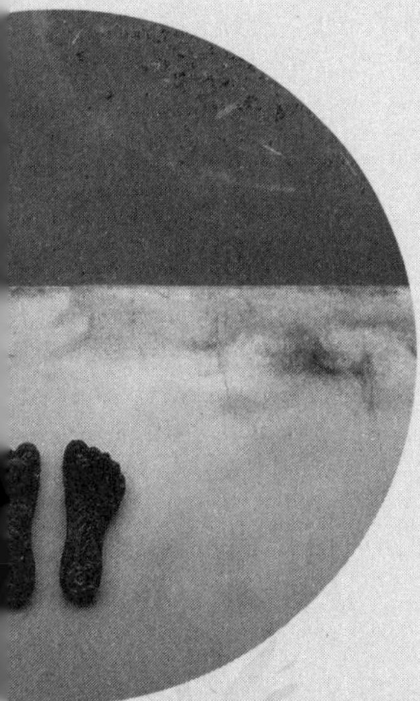

USS PAAR
THE OTHER SIDE

I am floating mindfully,

learning how not to turn ropes into snakes

THE RIVER AND THE BUS

I was back in Rishikesh, this time with P and C. It had been five years since I flew into Jolly Grant, and I was surprised to arrive at a totally different airport. It was posh and Singaporey, with shiny high ceilings and a fancy liquor shop, part of the New India that the government has conjured up as it propped up a Hindu Disneyland. I was impressed. But I also felt vaguely nostalgic for the shabby chic frugality that reflected a very Indian idea that you were never the owner, only a trustee, of material wealth.

Despite all the changes, and the hotchpotch vibe with signs for river rafting jostling with posters announcing meditation camps, Rishikesh remains fabulous. This time, we were not at the ashram but at a hillside hotel geared for adventure sport, in the Tehri Garhwal region of upper Rishikesh, along the Badrinath Road that follows the winding river through the foothills, all the way to its source.

I had swum in this divine bathtub, year after year. This was the first time we were doing it as a family. I had prayed for this. And the forces had gently guided me to this point, after extracting humility, patience and perseverance. I could almost see god smile as life gradually chipped away my ego and moved me towards a gentler, more grateful, version of myself.

Life works in interesting ways. The incense stick has to burn for its fragrance to spread. Finally, only the burnt rope of ash lingers, seemingly real in its physicality but, with one swift blow of breath, it too vanishes into thin air.

We swam in the icy river, at first shivering, then slowly easing into its crisp coldness. The winter sun sprinkled its silvery luminescence on the turquoise, like the shiny feathery varak on a piece of pistachio barfi. After swimming, dunking, praying, we lay on the white sandy banks, spreadeagled like stranded starfish. We were surrounded by millions of perfectly smooth stones that had rolled down the mountains over centuries, insentient, but on them we could read the story of mankind's futile and misguided attempts to control nature. Could even the most brilliant geologist ever know where a particular stone, say that purple-grey oval one with a white streak running diagonally across, was from? Or where it would end up? Was that stone once my neighbour in New York? The blonde man who loved mountain-climbing? Or did it hold the secret life of my great-great-great-great-grandmother?

Further north, cracks were developing in overbuilt mountain towns and landslides had become routine. The stones seemed to have more wisdom than humans. They seemed to be telling us, silently, that we did not exist outside nature; we are but one of its many elements. Human beings are actually quite inconsequential to the universal play of the elements. If they don't align to that larger play, humans will eventually be vanquished. So many stories, myths and symbols repeatedly remind us of this, but our foolish, myopic, egocentric minds have learnt to discard them as pointless, imaginative fluff.

There was a time when the earth was so parched that Bhagirath prayed for respite and requested help from the gods. Ganga, the river goddess, agreed to make her way down to quench the earth but was initially hesitant.

'Won't my pristine waters get dirty with the filth of humans? If I cleanse sinners, won't I absorb their sins?' she asked Brahma.

'Ganga, you are flowing through the feet of Vishnu. You will always remain pure.'

She tried to stall again, saying that the force of her landing would pierce the earth and split it in two. Brahma and Bhagirath knew she was trying to find a way to avoid earthly living. Finally, she herself found the solution and said she would descend into Shiva's labyrinthine locks to break the fall, and that is how she cascaded gently into the Himalayas, forming many tributaries.

We were in the lap of the Himalayas with the Ganga by our side.

The next day, we hopped on to a local bus that would take us north on the road that eventually goes to Badrinath, Kedarnath and beyond. The road meanders along the river, up and down the hills, passing shrines that evoke stories about mountain gods and goddesses. We were headed for Devprayag, where the ferocious Bhagirathi and the calmer Alakananda merge to become the Ganga. This unified river then flows down the mountains and across the plains, nourishing thousands, absorbing life, accepting death, and playing out many versions of its self before resolving into the Bay of Bengal.

The bus journey was more fun than the actual confluence, where we would find pilgrims loitering and taking selfies. A man in a brinjal-coloured monkey cap, seated next to me, spent the entire two-hour ride chatting in a monotonous drone to another fellow who appeared to be his subordinate in some government engineering department. The junior engineer was fighting to stay awake and feigned interest in his boss's stories, which were more like lectures. I entertained myself by eavesdropping, an old-time journalistic habit.

'What is maya?' the monkey-capped one asked Junior, speaking in enviably lyrical Hindustani. 'It is as fleeting and ephemeral as the mist that rises over the Ganga. It is the collective spell from which we have to disentangle ourselves, and understand the real reality.'

He droned on, unspooling the story of Narada, an ascetic who was famous for being the ultimate devotee to the god Vishnu. Now, Narada wanted desperately to penetrate the secret of maya, to understand what it really means. So, Vishnu appeared before him and they walked many miles together, under a blazing sun. At some point, Vishnu asked Narada to get him water, so Narada wandered off and came to a hut. When he knocked on the door, it was opened by a beautiful woman. He was so enchanted by her that he forgot why he had come there in the first place. As though in a daze, he went inside and started living with the family there and, shortly afterwards, married the woman who had captivated him. He became the head of the household, had several children, and eventually took on the responsibility of the farm and the cattle. Then, one day, torrential rains flooded the village and everyone had to escape to safety. Narada also left, holding his wife by one hand, a child by another, and carrying his youngest child on his shoulders through the slippery mud and swirling water in pitch darkness. The rain was so relentless and the current so strong that, at some point, he lost his entire family and fell unconscious. When he woke up, he saw muddy water all around him and started weeping.

Suddenly, he heard a familiar voice: 'Child, where is the water you went to fetch for me? I've been waiting for half an hour.'

When Narada turned around, there were no floods; he was back on the parched land with his companion, Vishnu, who said in a gentle tone: 'Do you now understand the secret of my maya, and how you became spellbound by it?'

At some point, lulled by the story and the bus ride, I dozed off, a privilege that was not available to the junior engineer. Like Narada, I also woke up and realised that I was listening to the tail end of the story. Was it real or part of my own dream? Row, row, row your boat gently down the stream ...

The man under the purple monkey cap was now lecturing his companion about psychology and how the conscious mind interacts with the collective unconscious. When my ears tuned into these English terms that had been thrown into the Hindi narrative, I roused myself to pay attention. I was astounded at the erudition in his storytelling. This person had clearly read a lot or been around some very learned people.

'You see, our individual conscious personality is the part that we call maya, but there is a vast, deep space that contains our unconscious mind which is collective and contains all the potentials and possibilities, past present and future, indiscriminate. You are both those …'

It was incredible. Here, on a winding bus ride to a spot where two rivers merge, I was listening to a conversation in which the cosmic and the individual were also merging. A garrulous Uttarakhand man wearing ugly headgear was unwittingly invoking Carl Jung, who had long ago suggested that myths are not primitive stories to entertain the naïve mind, but are involuntary revelations of the psyche. They take us, like enigmatic holograms, far beyond the limits of the human imagination, which is constantly seeking refuge in the boring, predictable intellect. They are not the quaint cartoon excursions we remember from our childhoods, sometimes poetic, at other times raw and savage; rather, they teach us about ourselves, challenging us to navigate the paradox of existence. These stories suggest that you can find wisdom in the most unlikely places, through a crow, or a man on a bus. Truth reveals itself occasionally, sometimes playfully, often momentarily, if you are open to receiving, and willing to pause and pay attention, like that miniature painting of a tree with white flowers falling to the ground, revealing Krishna.

So many of our fellow passengers, ordinary people on a bus, seem to have grown up with some version of faith or wisdom that remains with them, perhaps derived from a grandfather, or their own readings, or wherever stories come from. This vast, remarkably fluid treasury of stories, myths and epics are actually leading towards a very powerful unifying idea: that there is a universe operating way beyond anything our organs of perception and our mind can possibly reveal or grasp.

It is astonishing that this idea has also been espoused by many physicists who suggest that every word or concept has only a limited range of applicability. We need them to make sense of reality, but they are limited and relative. As Fritjof Capra said, 'don't mistake the map for the territory'. 'The mystic and the physicist arrive at the same conclusion; one starting from the inner realm, the other from the outer world.* The harmony between their views confirms the ancient Indian wisdom that Brahman, the ultimate reality without, is identical to Atman, the reality within'.** The quantum physicist Werner Heisenberg said: 'The first gulp from the glass of natural sciences will turn you into an atheist, but at the bottom of the glass, god is waiting for you.' We have to constantly remind ourselves that our concepts and constructs of reality are easier to grasp than reality itself, that they are not reality. A simple example is time. Is time real or relative? Time is a construct that can be broken down into unit after unit after unit. Then what? Shiva, in the form of Kaala Bhairava, swallowed time.

Listening to the man on the bus, I was reminded of the time when I was on a train to Shimla and met a young man who worked in an organisation that researched potatoes. He chatted with me about the riddles that the yaksha asked Yudhishtira long after the war of Mahabharata was over. He said it was one of his favourite parts of the epic.

1. What is more fleeting than the wind and more numerous than grass?

---

* From *The Tao of Physics by Fritjof Capra*, published by Shambhala Publications, 1975.

** Ibid.

2. Who is the best friend of one about to die?
3. Who is truly happy?
4. What is the greatest riddle of the universe?

Give some thought to these questions, I later tell C. Stay suspended in earnest contemplation before attempting any answers. We will come back to them because we have to be patient. It is one of the secret ingredients in a journey where time is not of the essence, where the destination cannot be found on Google maps.

As we went further up towards Devprayag, a passenger motioned to the bus conductor. He, in turn, signalled to the driver to stop. Two passengers got off holding small woven mats, laid them on the ground by the side of the road, and knelt to pray. Another man got off, stretched, and sat cross-legged on a boulder, staring at the distant mountains, his version of prayer. I was surprised that no one protested over the unscheduled stop, perhaps upholding community over individual? Or was it because of the understanding that there was no need to hurry because time is, after all, a construct, and we are all essentially hurtling towards the same inevitable destination? I didn't know the answer. But I allowed myself the indulgence of possibilities. I firmly believe that, in India, the abiding language of communication is spiritual, despite periodic hiccups of hatred.

All around us, there had been alarming news about how cracks had developed on houses in the town of Joshimath and on the Badrinath road. I was sad to see how people who had grown up in a land of such wisdom, who prayed to the sun every morning and the river every afternoon had also lost their way, driven by an anthropocentric version of progress and development that defied the forces of nature. Like the mountaineer who aspired to 'conquer' peaks and realised too late, caught in a fatal snowstorm, that mountains have their own mystery and power.

We reached Devprayag at five in the evening, just before the magical hour that is neither day nor night, and hopped off the bus. There, in front of us, was the confluence that had birthed India's most beloved river. Bubbling down from the Gaumukh glacier was the pale blue Bhagirathi, named after the devout king who had brought water to this land. And on the other side, almost still in its gentle flow, came the muddy Alakananda. The two meet and continue to flow on their separate journeys, respectfully, side by side, the two different colours still clearly demarcated, not intruding on each other's space, like an enlightened couple, and then seamlessly merge to enter the infinite ocean. There is resolution. There is peace.

The answers to the yaksha's questions are:

1. What is more fleeting than the wind and more numerous than grass?
   Your thoughts.
2. Who is the best friend of one about to die?
   A prayer beyond desire, which reaches out to the open sky.
3. Who is truly happy?

That man who doesn't stir from home, cooks his own meals, isn't in debt and is happy to be alone.

4. What is the greatest riddle of the universe?

   Millions pass on, yet the living live their lives as if they will never die. What can be more wonderful than this wonderful lie?

   As Yudhishtira says: 'In this cauldron fashioned from delusion, with the sun as fire, and day and night as kindling wood, the months and seasons as the ladle for stirring, Time (or death) cooks all beings. This is the simple truth.'

WALKING EACH OTHER HOME

You never step into the same river twice. Namita, who first tentatively stepped into the Ganga ten years ago, was a different Namita from the one who was floating in it now, bobbing with the ease of a middle-aged river dolphin. The old masks had floated down the water and disappeared like transient bubbles. There was only lightness, buoyancy.

Every moment passes, and your only reality is the present moment. That is freedom. That is where your attention must be. Even the past is actually remembered only in the present moment, filtered through a sieve of selective nostalgia.

I had begun to trust something higher than myself.

There is a big picture that is gloriously ordered and perfect: the photosynthesis endlessly in motion in the garden, the rhythm of moon phases, the blood that is pulsating through my body without me doing anything, these are all majestically, meticulously ordered. By that logic, none of us is outside this order, and no individual or situation is random. I am a tiny dot in that big picture. Everything is a medium that helps align me with it. I now keep joining the flower-dots and seeing the colossal Krishna.

You cannot see this picture through your senses, only through wisdom. You have to first wipe the mirror clean. Your superpower lies in not taking things personally, not feeling defensive when something does not go your way, because you are truly *truly* not in a position to get the bird's eye view on your life. You are a small piece in this complex, interconnected web that is operating far beyond your small, individuated self. What a relief, to not have to keep pushing round circles into square holes.

In short, you are not the centre of the universe, you are a part of it. The Isha Upanishad says:

> *Those who see all creatures in themselves*
> *And themselves in all creatures know no fear*
> *Those who see all creatures in themselves*
> *And themselves in all creatures know no grief.*
> *How can the multiplicity of life*
> *Delude the one who sees its unity?**

When a person does what they appear to be doing *to* you, it is not about you alone. There are multiple things taking place—that person has a back story which influences how they think and act; you also have a back story that colours the way you receive information. Broken down, most interactions between human beings are essentially one person's nervous system with all its unresolved issues reacting to another's nervous system! Arguments take place

* From *The Upanishads* by Eknath Easwaran, published by Jaico Books, 2010.

between one ego construct and another, both of which have a limited or disjointed view, while the 'is' of life carries on, based on so many factors way beyond anyone's control. You, the true self, are far beyond the drama.

In our world, there are multiple things taking place simultaneously and each comes with its own independent narrative. But the human mind—in its obsessive attempts to rationalise, compartmentalise and make sense of things—starts superimposing a narrative.

Here is an example. You are sitting under a tree. The sun is setting. A bird on a tree suddenly dies and falls on your head. Now, the bird did not die because of you, or because the sun had just set. It died because it was time for it to die. It fell, and you happened to be sitting there and the sun was then setting. There is no connection between the three events other than timing. There are a gazillion such events taking place at exactly the same time with their disparate yet interconnected narratives. Yet, so self-absorbed are we that we take everything personally, and that could lead to distress, fear, even war.

We tell ourselves stories, and when someone's story does not match with our own story, we feel dissonance. Stories help navigate grey areas, as long as I do not make myself the centre of the story. The minute I step out, become the observer of the 'movie', I am able to witness the complex and constantly morphing cosmos. Once I understand this, how can I then believe that a perceived moment of chaos in my life would be outside that order? It is not even logical! I am a mere piece in the drama—a unique moment in an infinity that has neither beginning nor end. My eventual goal is to recognise the consciousness that abides beyond individual perceptions and stories. That is the real story beyond the story.

The Mundaka Upanishad says that just as a spider spins its web from its own juice, we create our world, move around in it, and then pull it back in ... 'We are like the dreamer who dreams and then lives in the dream.' We spin stories like a spider on amphetamines. Our minds constantly and repeatedly project these stories on ourselves, on other people, on events, sometimes amplifying soft notes into jarring rock concerts. We enable our thoughts to manipulate and gaslight us into a slow burn state of almost-insanity.

We turn ropes into snakes.

Everything starts changing once you mute your ego and its web-spinning machine and use the relative ego-self only to understand the absolute self. The wisdom of the rishis makes it easier to understand that you are a spiritual being trying to be human, not the other way around. You continue to live in the circus, but viewing life in a panoramic sense, a less self-absorbed perspective. Every person—parent, sibling, spouse, stranger—is in your life as an instrument to teach you. Their purpose could be to help you follow in their footsteps or it could even be to become the opposite of them.

Is it possible to experience love in abstraction, regard-less of the object of love? Love is compassion and understanding. That is our true nature.

I now believe that everything happens for a reason and you have to decode the lesson. Life is a game of snakes and ladders so, even after you have been bitten by a snake, you can churn the poison into nectar. You try and develop a more neutral approach, rather than opining one way or another.

This is. Not, this is unfortunate or fantastic or terrible or fabulous. Situations and people come into your life to teach you, not negate you.

Don't come in the way of your self.

❧

In my early twenties, when I was living in New York, I fell in love—twice. First, with books. I was working at Alfred Knopf under its charismatic publisher Sonny Mehta, though all I did was photocopy manuscripts. The second time was with a young man called P, or maybe it was with what he was instrumental in bringing to me.

It was a Saturday evening and we were in a little apartment on the Upper East Side when, suddenly, this boisterous non-yogi-ish man started talking about the rope and the snake—how we are constantly mistaking the rope for a snake, and stumbling through life because we rely only on our senses to understand things.

'Don't confuse the map for the land,' he said, or something like that.

I had never heard this kind of chatter. It struck something deep within. I was intrigued. I wanted more. My handsome classmate was also some sort of philosopher? I kept listening to him until it was time for us to head downtown to listen to the blues.

Later that evening, he held my hand and said: 'In the end, we are all just walking each other home.'

❧

Om Purnamadah Purnamidam
Purnat Purnamudachyate
Purnasya Purnamadaya
Purnameva Avashishyate

All this is whole, All that is whole
From wholeness, wholeness arises
If we take away wholeness from wholeness
Wholeness still remains.

This is one of Mahatma Gandhi's favourite prayers, from the Isha Upanishad.

This universe is complete, whole and perfect. We humans are born of the universe and are, therefore, also complete, whole and perfect. Every single thing in the universe, sentient and insentient, has come from one common source, will return to that, and contains that fullness. You Are That.

Pay attention to the sound of the water.

Pay attention to the sound of no sound.

ACKNOWLEDGEMENTS

Solitude has been biggest my partner on this journey, but a number of people have been fellow travellers or thoughtful readers.

Thanks first to my parents Meera and Bhagwat Devidayal for being such solid pillars. My in-laws, the Motwanes, who have equally nourished me. Shona Bulchandani helped me find my way to Rishikesh where my journey began. Vishwas Kulkarni nudged me to bring humour and pop into a book on spirituality. Thank you, Pratish Motwane, for serving up filterless coffee and forcing me to taste life in all its raw, dark, unadulterated splendour.

Readers who have given me valuable inputs include Arshia Sattar, Bijoy Jain, Gayatri Yadav, Jaishree Goyal, Kehan Shetty, Laleh Dubash, Naheed Carrimjee, Nandini Mirani, Nilanjana Roy, Meenal Baghel, Pavan K. Varma, Ranjit Hoskote, Rishad Suntook, Saloni Jhaveri, Shanta Gokhale, Siddharth Roy Kapur, Sujoy Chohan and Sunil Mirani.

An enormous thank you to my editors Karthika V.K. and Ajitha G.S., who gently skimmed the fat off the book. And thank you Westland Books for believing in me again.

Much of my understanding of Vedanta philosophy has come from listening to the classes taught by Neema Majmudar, which gave me clarity and the confidence to write on this subject. I have also been inspired by the following books:

The Gospel of Sri Ramakrishna
Value of Values by Swami Dayananda Saraswati
The Great Hindu Civilisation by Pavan K. Varma
The Upanishads by Sri Aurobindo
The Upanishads by Eknath Easwaran
Be Here Now by Ram Dass
Mahagatha by Satyarth Nayak
Discovering Love by Swami Dayananda Saraswati
Maha Yoga by K. Lakshmana Sarma
Myths and Symbols in Indian Art and Civilisation by Heinrich Zimmer
Yoga Vasishta by Swami Venkatesananda

I have liberally quoted lyrics from some of my favourite musicians—Grateful Dead, Beatles, Bob Dylan, Crosby, Stills, Nash & Young, Pink Floyd, and more.

Thank you, my beloved son Chaitanya Motwane, who has the equanimity of a morning raga and gave me the best literary advice: 'Mom, don't give gyaan. Just tell your story ...'

In fact, we are all a bunch of self-fashioned stories.

With the same ending.